高校英语选修课系列教材

A COURSEBOOK OF CULTURALLY SPOKEN ENGLISH FOR APPLIED COLLEGES

应用型大学英语文化口语教程

主　编　杨　梅　高朝阳

副主编　张晓红　田孟鑫

编　者　李雨虹　常　伟　钟　虹
　　　　牟利璘　晏　雪　吴林兵
　　　　田　野

U0360517

清华大学出版社

北　京

内 容 简 介

本教材以应用型本科院校的人才培养为目标,充分考虑应用型本科院校学生的实际英语口语水平和学习需求,重点培养学生的文化阐释能力和文化思辨能力。全书共6个单元,话题是学生感兴趣的绿色生活、爱的真谛、友谊、留学生活、创客运动和科技发展,富于人文关怀和思辨性。单元内设计了丰富有趣的口语活动,如角色扮演、小组讨论、图片描述等,旨在鼓励学生积极参与口语表达。教材配有学生录制的音视频,供学生参考学习,读者可登录www.tsinghuaelt.com下载使用。

本教材可作为应用型本科院校大学英语基础课、选修课教材,也可作为口语练习材料,供学生自学。

图书在版编目(CIP)数据

应用型大学英语文化口语教程 / 杨梅,高朝阳主编. ——北京:清华大学出版社,2024.5(2024.8重印)
高校英语选修课系列教材
ISBN 978-7-302-66229-7

Ⅰ.①应… Ⅱ.①杨… ②高… Ⅲ.①英语—口语—高等学校—教材 Ⅳ.①H319.32

中国国家版本馆CIP数据核字(2024)第096761号

责任编辑:刘 艳
封面设计:平 原
责任校对:王荣静
责任印制:沈 露
出版发行:清华大学出版社
　　网　　　址:https://www.tup.com.cn, https://www.wqxuetang.com
　　地　　　址:北京清华大学学研大厦A座　　邮　　编:100084
　　社 总 机:010-83470000　　　　　　　　邮　　购:010-62786544
　　投稿与读者服务:010-62776969, c-service@tup.tsinghua.edu.cn
　　质量反馈:010-62772015, zhiliang@tup.tsinghua.edu.cn
印 装 者:北京嘉实印刷有限公司
经　　销:全国新华书店
开　　本:185mm×260mm　　印　　张:9.75　　字　　数:197千字
版　　次:2024 年 5 月第 1 版　　　　　　印　　次:2024 年 8 月第 2 次印刷
定　　价:52.00元

产品编号:103970-01

前言
Preface

　　《大学英语教学指南》（2020 版）指出，大学英语课程在"培养学生对中国文化的理解和阐释能力，服务中国文化对外传播"方面发挥着重要作用。党的二十大报告也首次提出要"增强中华文明传播力、影响力""讲好中国故事、传播好中国声音，展现可信、可爱、可敬的中国形象"。应用型本科院校的大学英语课程旨在培养学生学习与专业相关的学术英语或职业英语，获得在专业学术或职业领域进行国际交流的能力，同时注重培养学生的思辨能力和对外传播中国文化的能力。对大多数学生来说，能较为熟练地使用英语表达自己的想法和观点，对外进行交流沟通是最迫切的需求。

　　针对这一需求，我们编写了这本《应用型大学英语文化口语教程》。本教材有以下特点：

　　话题人文思辨色彩浓厚：本教材共 6 个单元，话题涉及学生感兴趣的绿色生活、爱的真谛、友谊、留学生活、创客运动和科技发展，富于人文关怀，更能激发学生参与讨论的兴趣和积极性，培养他们的思辨能力。

　　口语活动丰富有趣：每个单元都设计了一系列互动性强的活动，比如角色扮演、小组讨论、图片描述等，旨在鼓励学生积极参与口语表达，锻炼真实情境下的口语表达能力。同时，本教材还注重批判性思维能力的培养，活动设计层层递进，逐步引导学生对单元话题进行深度思考，形成独立的见解。另外，教材还提供了由学生录制的相关音视频资源供学生学习参考。

　　本教材可作为应用型本科院校大学英语基础课、选修课教材，也可作为口语练习材料，供学生自学使用。希望本教材能够有效帮助学生达到应用型本科人才培养的要求，提高文化思辨和英语口语交流能力。

　　在编写过程中，本教材得到了攀枝花学院李静波老师和刘烨老师的大力支持，她们为本教材的编写提供了丰富的资料。同时，攀枝花学院 2020 级至 2023 级部分学生参与了配套音视频资源的录制，他们是田丹、汪骏、杨洋、刘婧、崔杨、黄贞、陈饶、周雪、杨梦、

罗崇高、邹思思、谢怡婷、甯文霞、唐建军、胡彩丽、刘思怡、李思琪、宋燕君、李林燕、朱虹润、郑诗瑶、申脐秀、彭诗雨、王松林、刘定鑫、高梦蝶、许玉珠、姚诗佳、罗宇欣、瞿彭阳扬，在此一并表示诚挚的感谢。

　　由于编者水平有限，书中难免有不足之处，恳请读者批评指正。

编者

2024 年 4 月

目录
Contents

Unit 1
Living Green

Warm-up Questions

① What does "living green" mean?
② What are your tips for living green?
③ What's the significance of living green?

Section A   Getting Ready to Speak

Part One

Read the following topic-related passages and answer the questions accordingly.

What Does "Living Green" Mean?

Living green means having a lifestyle that is environmentally conscious. It means being Earth-friendly or environmentally friendly, rather than doing things that are harmful to our world. In general, living green can be accomplished through doing what is known as "the 3 Rs": reducing, reusing, and recycling.

Reducing waste helps lower the amount of garbage in landfills. Garbage that is piled up causes pollution; it's difficult to dispose of it cleanly and some of it ends up in the oceans. Some groups focusing on green living have protested the amount of packaging that manufacturers use in making products, such as having an item in a box with plastic wrap over it. Many companies today have new packaging designs that are more environmentally friendly, resulting in less waste.

One of the most important ways of living green is to reduce carbon emissions from vehicles. Emissions from cars are a big threat to sustainable living. Environmental sustainability refers to the maintenance of resources for healthy living to continue. It's a known fact that if we continue to pollute the Earth, it will no longer be a sustainable environment for future generations. Besides driving less, buying food locally rather than having it transported from long distances is another way of participating in green living by helping to reduce carbon emissions.

Reusing items helps keep them from piling up in the landfill. Donating still usable, but unwanted clothing and household goods to people or organizations allows the items to have a second life rather than having to be processed as garbage. Reusing stained or ripped clothing as cleaning rags is another way of living green. In addition to being reused, cloth rags cut down or eliminate the amount of paper towels needed in a household. Unless they're made from recycled materials, paper towels aren't considered environmentally friendly as the pulp they consist of comes from natural resources including trees.

Many companies today are more environmentally conscious than they were in the past decades. Some manufacturers choose greener methods for producing goods, while others use recycled materials. Using recycled paper products made for the kitchen and bathroom that earth-conscious companies produce is a part of living green today.

Most cities have recycling programs in which residents not only place garbage out for pickup but items that can be recycled rather than sent to the landfill. Bins can be used to store glass bottles, newspapers, plastic containers, and many other recyclable goods in the home until pickup day. Living green means never throwing anything into the garbage before considering whether it can be recycled. Container manufacturers today place numbers on items such as margarine tubs and inserts that hold commercial cookies or crackers so that consumers know whether certain product containers are recyclable.

Question 1: Through what ways can living green be accomplished?

Question 2: In what ways can waste be reduced to help us live green?

Exchange of Goods

Of the rash of bartering sites that appeared in 2006, only a few survive. But their patrons believe money-less exchange is the way forward for a green lifestyle.

In 2006, Canadian blogger Kyle MacDonald, who bartered his way from a single red paper clip to a house, through a series of online trades became a much-told tale. Shanghai native Li Huizhu has swapped coupons and show tickets given by the nursery school where she teaches, and cosmetics gifted by friends and colleagues, for more than 500 items of everyday use. This has helped her accumulate all the shampoo and soaps her family has needed over the two years that she has been bartering. "Everything, except for money, is exchangeable on the bartering website. All you do is to upload a picture of the items you don't want, write a few words about it, leave your contact information, and then, just wait and see what happens," says Li. "The only rule to follow is to be honest with what you deal. Don't brag about or hide anything. And keep in mind the item's utility for the other side," Li adds.

But Sun Yumin, one of the founders of a Shanghai-based bartering website, and Li's friend, believes successful bartering calls for "a special talent"—a combination of a salesman's persuasiveness and a collector's shrewdness. "Bartering is based on trust. There is never a guarantee of satisfaction. And conflicts occur frequently, especially when it comes to electronic gadgets," Sun says. To minimize troubles, the swapping of goods is usually done face-to-face, so that the items can be examined personally before a deal is sealed. These personal meetings also lead to unlikely friendships. "Girls and boys at my son's age come to me for help with telling fakes from originals, and secondhand from new. I feel young and happy hanging out with them," Li says. According to Sun, 70% of the website's members are young white-collar workers, with retired or middle-aged computer-literate people comprising the rest. The most popular items are discount shopping cards, bakery coupons, and show tickets that have a precise value.

Hundreds of bartering websites cropped up in 2007 when the legend of Kyle MacDonald swept through the country. But most were unable to turn in a profit and shut down. Since they provide a free service for those users, some sites make money only through advertisements posted by other online stores, and that is often just enough to offset its basic costs. The only reason for its survival, Sun says, is that it is free. That leaves little scope for any expansion, in spite of its increasing popularity.

Question 1: What's your understanding of bartering sites?

Question 2: What's the purpose of exchanging goods on the bartering website?

18 Tips for Environmental Protection

Each and every one of us is responsible for the greenhouse gases we emit in our daily actions and choices. Therefore, combating climate change is going to take the combined efforts of everyone on the planet.

The average household carbon footprint in China is 2.41 tons of carbon dioxide annually. That's enough to fill half an Olympic swimming pool.

Surprised? Well, here's how you can work to reduce it:

1. Take showers rather than baths and reduce your shower time by two minutes. This will save water and give you an extra two minutes in bed.

2. Don't purchase unnecessary clothes, and be careful about the materials you buy. Wool and cotton fabrics have a really high greenhouse gas impact. Man-made fibers such as polyester are a better choice.

3. There's no point having the heat up high while the wind is blowing in under the door or sneaking in through the window. Reseal all window frames to keep the heat in.

4. Try to buy high-quality, long-lasting products even though they may cost a little more. A laptop is more efficient than a desktop, and a small-screen TV is better than a big flat-screen.

5. Only turn the water heater on when necessary, and adjust temperature controls to avoid overheating. Put a lid on a pan when boiling water.

6. When using the washing machine, be sure there's a full load and turn the temperature down if it's not really grubby.

7. The greediest home device along with the washing machine is the fridge. Make sure it's as efficient as possible by keeping it out of direct sunlight and away from the oven or heater.

8. This is obvious, but essential: switch off all appliances when you're not using them. This includes lights.

9. Conserve energy by using efficient light bulbs. They use about one-third of the energy of normal bulbs and last 10 times as long.

10. Only print things out when necessary, and print double-sided and reduce the margins.

11. Take your own mug and cutlery to work. This saves throwing away disposable cups and containers—but that could be outweighed by washing your cutlery. So, pay attention to how you use water when washing your dishes.

12. Find out what the recycling options are in your area. Then make sure you keep items such as paper and plastic bottles separate so that they can be recycled. There are places where you can recycle electronic appliances and batteries. Make sure you find them.

13. Look for reusable, recyclable, and biodegradable items and remember to carry your reusable shopping bags.

14. Each week, choose one day when you don't eat meat. Meat uses up lots of energy because it takes a long time to produce.

15. Only buy the amount of food you need and if there are leftovers, get creative. For instance, make them into a soup. Ask to take food home from restaurants if there's some left, but remember to take your own container to avoid using a disposable carton.

16. Food production eats up lots of energy. When you buy food, go local rather than imported, and get fresh vegetables instead of frozen.

17. All motorized travel is carbon-intensive. Buses and trains are better than cars, but walking or cycling is better still. It's also better for your health and cheaper.

18. Air travel is an environmental disaster. As well as carbon dioxide, planes emit nitrogen oxide, another nasty gas.

Question 1: What can you do to reduce the greenhouse gases emitted in daily life?

Question 2: What else can you do to protect the environment?

Part Two

Act out the following dialogs with your partner. Change the role when necessary.

Jean: Hey, Helen, what are you up to?

Helen: Hi, Jean, I'm browsing TikTok.

Jean: Oh, which short video are you watching?

Helen: A local one. It's about recycling old clothes. I have a lot of old clothes, and I'm considering reaching out to the person who posted the video.

Jean: Really? I also have a bunch of old clothes and don't know what to do with them. Please share it with me.

Helen: No problem. Recycling can contribute to environmental protection. In addition to old clothes, items like glass, paper, plastics, cardboard, and tin cans can be taken to a recycling center to reduce resource waste.

Jean: I had no idea you were so environmentally conscious!

Helen: Honestly, if we want the Earth to remain a habitable place, we all need to take a greater interest in the environment.

Jean: Yes, our environment used to be beautiful. The air was fresh, the water was clean, the sky was blue, and so on.

Helen: There are many things we can do to protect our environment.

Jean: Yes, we should start with small and everyday things. For example, using fewer disposable chopsticks, opting for eco-friendly transportation, and more.

Helen: Caring for flowers, protecting birds and animals, saving water, and properly managing resources…

Jean: The first step is the TikTok short video. Have you shared it with me?

Helen: Certainly. I sent it to you as soon as you asked.

Jean: OK, thank you.

Helen: You're welcome.

Jean: Now, I'm heading to the library. See you.

Helen: See you.

A: Hi Nancy, did you also come to listen to the Energy and Sustainable Development report?

B: Yes. What are your thoughts on this report?

A: I think I learned a lot. As we all know, with the development of society, various energy sources such as coal, petroleum, and natural gas have been extensively used. However, the availability of these energy sources is limited. The unchecked consumption of energy resources has led to an energy crisis.

B: Yes, you're right. Since the first "energy crisis" in 1973–1974, it has occurred several times. The economies of some developing countries heavily reliant on petroleum have been severely impacted by energy crises.

A: Fossil fuel resources, like coal, unlike sunlight, are not renewable within the scope of human history. Once depleted, they are gone forever. Moreover, the substantial pollution caused by coal is also a significant concern.

B: Therefore, it is evident that finding solutions to the "energy crisis" and pursuing sustainable development are crucial. Many measures have been proposed to conserve existing energy resources and explore new ones.

A: Yes, I believe developing new forms of energy is imperative. This includes wind power, solar energy, hydroelectric power, nuclear fusion power, and hydrogen gas.

B: Consequently, the field of energy engineering has emerged and developed. Its primary focus is to identify methods to reduce energy consumption while maintaining or even increasing output. Additionally, determining the most effective means of reducing energy usage is also essential.

A: This way, we can adopt a low-carbon lifestyle. "Low-carbon" has become a frequently used and trendy term lately. Living a low-carbon life refers to a lifestyle where individuals make an effort to minimize energy consumption and greenhouse gas emissions.

B: Yes, how can we live a low-carbon life? I believe, firstly, we need to understand that it is not merely a lifestyle choice but also an attitude towards life. Each of us is responsible for the greenhouse gases emitted through our everyday actions. Secondly, developing good habits in our daily lives is crucial.

A: Indeed, all forms of motorized travel contribute to carbon emissions. Buses and trains are better than cars, but walking or cycling is the most eco-friendly option.

Tom: Hi, Jack!

Jack: Hi, Tom!

Tom: It's freezing today!

Jack: Yeah, but don't you feel like this winter is warmer compared with previous years?

Tom: Absolutely! I think the primary reason behind this is the greenhouse effect, which has been causing the Earth to gradually warm up.

Jack: That's a valid point! As inhabitants of Earth, it's our collective responsibility to take action and protect our planet. If we don't, our living environment will only deteriorate further.

Tom: Living a low-carbon life is crucial. It should be our top priority.

Jack: Absolutely, "green living" has become a popular term in recent years. Not just China, all countries are focusing on the concept of "low-carbon".

Tom: That's true. With increasing air pollution, water pollution, and chemical pollution, our living environment is worsening day by day.

Jack: That's why we need to safeguard our planet, the only place that provides us with a livable environment. "Low-carbon living" has emerged as a new and innovative lifestyle. Do you

happen to know when the term "low-carbon life" was first mentioned?

Tom: Yes, of course. It was first mentioned at the Copenhagen Summit. It can be understood as a lifestyle that aims to reduce carbon dioxide emissions and use resources efficiently. Its purpose is to raise awareness and protect our environment. Living a low-carbon life should not just be a slogan; it needs to be put into practice.

Jack: Absolutely. We should develop good habits of low-carbon living in our daily lives, like recycling old batteries, using energy-saving light bulbs, and turning off power sockets when not in use. Moreover, we need to actively encourage those around us to embrace a low-carbon lifestyle.

Tom: Spreading the message of low-carbon living not only helps to reduce emissions and contribute to our cities but also benefits us personally, such as maintaining good health and setting positive examples for future generations.

Jack: It's a long-term commitment, and everyone should be dedicated to it.

Tom: Indeed, we must start now and lead by example.

Jack: That's right. Look! The lights in that classroom seem to be left on.

Tom: Yeah, I see. Let's go and begin our low-carbon life right away.

Jack: Alright, let's go.

Part Three

Read the following useful expressions and finish the matching exercise that follows.

- accumulation of radioactive waste　放射性废料积存
- acid rain and transboundary air pollution　酸雨和越境空气污染
- afforestation project　造林工程
- afforested area / greening space　绿化面积
- air pollution concentration　空气污染浓度
- atmospheric monitoring system　大气监测系统
- carrying capacity of environment　环境负荷
- cell-driven vehicle / battery car　电动汽车

- centralized treatment plant 集中处理厂
- clean energy 清洁能源
- conservation of water and soil 水土保持
- conserve natural habitats 保护自然栖息地
- curb environmental pollution / bring the pollution under control 治理环境污染
- decontamination rate of urban refuse 城市垃圾无害化处理率
- desertification 沙漠化 / 荒漠化
- develop renewable resources 开发可再生资源
- eco-demonstration region / environmental-friendly region 生态示范区
- endangered wildlife 濒危野生动物
- environmental degradation 环境恶化
- environmental-friendly agriculture / eco-agriculture 生态农业
- environmental-friendly product 环保产品
- exhaust purifier 尾气净化器
- fast-growing trees 速生林
- forest coverage 森林覆盖率
- fossil fuels (e.g., coal, oil, and natural gas) 矿物燃料（如煤、石油、天然气）
- gas-fueled vehicle 天然气汽车
- greenhouse effect 温室效应
- impact on the quality of water and air 对水质和空气质量的影响
- industrial dust discharged 排放的工业粉尘
- industrial solid wastes 工业固体废物
- International Biodiversity Day (29 December) 国际生物多样性日
- landscaping design for environmental purposes 环保景观设计
- lead-free gasoline 无铅汽油
- motor vehicle exhaust 汽车尾气排放
- multipurpose use of three types of wastes 三废综合利用
- National Tree-planting Day 全民义务植树日

- Nationally Designated Eco-demonstration Region 国家级生态示范区
- Nationally Designated Garden City 国家级园林城市
- natural ecosystem 自然生态系统
- nature reserve 自然保护区
- nitrate dioxide (NO_2) emission 二氧化氮排放
- organic pollutant 有机污染物
- pesticide residue 农药残留
- protect coral reefs, mangroves, and fishing resources 保护珊瑚礁、红树林和渔业资源
- protect forests from over exploitation 防止过度利用森林
- rare and endangered species breeding center 珍稀濒危物种繁育基地
- rate of deforestation 森林砍伐率
- red tide (rapid propagation of sea algae) 赤潮
- refuse incinerator 垃圾焚化厂
- refuse landfill 垃圾填埋场
- sand breaks 防沙林
- sea water desalinization 海水淡化
- slow down the rate of resource degradation 降低资源消耗率
- soil alkalization 土壤盐碱化
- soot emission 烟尘排放
- State Environmental Protection Administration (SEPA) 国家环境保护总局
- sulfur dioxide (SO_2) emission 二氧化硫排放
- suspended particles 悬浮颗粒物
- bio-degradable plastic bags 可生物降解塑料袋
- treatment rate of domestic sewage 城市污水处理率
- treatment rate of industrial effluent 工业废水处理率
- uncontrolled urbanization 城市化失控
- water and soil erosion 水土流失

- water resource conservation zone 水资源保护区
- white pollution (using and littering non-degradable white plastics) 白色污染
- wild fauna and flora 野生动植物
- wind breaks 防风林
- World Environment Day (5 June) 世界环境日（6月5日）
- World Meteorological Day (23 March) 世界气象日（3月23日）
- World Oceans Day (8 June) 世界海洋日（6月8日）
- World Water Day (22 March) 世界水日（3月22日）
- A green and low-carbon economy and society are crucial to high-quality development. 绿色、低碳的经济和社会对高质量发展至关重要。
- By advocating for more supportive policies to reduce dependence on automobiles through initiatives such as additional bike lanes, walking paths, and better public transportation options, we can live a greener life. 通过提倡更多支持性政策来减少对汽车的依赖，比如额外的自行车道和人行道以及更好的公共交通出行，我们可以过上更加绿色的生活。
- All energy needs for homes, shops, and office buildings should be met with renewable sources, with food waste converted to biogas to run local buses as much as possible. 家庭、商店和办公楼的所有能源需求应该由可再生资源来满足，将食物废料转化为沼气，尽可能多地用于地方公交车的运行。
- China will see its market-oriented green technology innovation system further improved by 2025, achieving stronger support from green technology innovation for the country's green and low-carbon development. 到2025年，中国将进一步完善市场导向的绿色科技创新体系，为国家的绿色低碳发展提供更强有力的支持。
- China will strike a balance between low-carbon transition and ensuring the living needs of its people, and between development and carbon reduction, and will achieve carbon peak and carbon neutrality within the time frame we set. 中国将在低碳转型与保障人民生活需求、发展与碳减排之间取得平衡，并在

我们设定的时间期限内实现碳达峰和碳中和。

- Don't throw away old clothes and books. Other people can reuse our unwanted clothes and books if we donate them. 不要扔掉旧衣服和旧书。如果我们把不需要的衣服和书籍捐出去，其他人可以重复使用它们。

- Everything from lights and ceiling fans to computers and radios is left on when they are not in use. The cellphone chargers are plugged in even when they aren't charging anything. All of these use unnecessary power. We are steadily learning to be more diligent with our power usage. 生活中有许多东西在不使用时也保持着开启状态，比如电灯、吊扇、电脑和收音机。甚至手机充电器不在充电时也插着。所有这些都浪费了不必要的电力，因此我们需要逐渐学会更加节约用电。

- Many things that we use are recyclable. If we get a container to collect the recyclable things, we can contribute to the conservation of natural resources and reduce the amount of pollution and greenhouse gas generated. 我们使用的许多物品都是可回收利用的。如果我们有一个容器来收集可回收利用的物品，就可以为自然资源保护做出贡献，从而减少污染物和温室气体的排放量。

- By purchasing new fuel-efficient automobiles, driving less than we used to, and shopping with our bike trailer, we intend to continue our family's efforts to live more sustainably. 通过购买燃油效率更高的新汽车、减少开车的次数以及使用自行车拖车购物，我们全家人打算继续过上更加可持续的生活。

- Solar water heaters would be immensely popular since they would help dramatically lower our energy costs while cutting carbon emissions. 太阳能热水器将非常受欢迎，因为它们不仅可以显著降低能源成本，而且可以减少碳排放。

- The central bank also requires those financial institutions to publicly disclose information on the carbon-reduction loans and the emission cuts financed by such loans. Third-party professional institutions will verify such information. 中央银行还要求这些金融机构公开披露关于减碳贷款和这些贷款资助与减排相关的信息。第三方专业机构将验证这些信息。

- These effective measures will bring us bluer skies, greener mountains, and cleaner waters. 这些有效措施将给我们带来更蓝的天空、更绿的山脉和更清洁的水域。

- To boost the development of the hydrogen fuel-cell vehicle industry will be another important method on the way to green, low-carbon, and sustainable development. 促进氢燃料电池车辆产业的发展将是走向绿色、低碳、可持续发展的另一种重要方法。

- We have acted on the idea that lucid waters and lush mountains are invaluable assets. 我们实践了"绿水青山就是金山银山"的理念。

- We have persisted with a holistic and systematic approach to conserving and improving mountain, water, forest, farmland, grassland, and desert ecosystems. 我们坚持用整体性和系统性的方法来保护和改善山地、水域、森林、耕地、草地和沙漠的生态系统。

- We should take care not to take electric power for granted. When we leave a room, all the lights should be turned off. 我们不应该认为电是理所当然存在的。当我们离开房间时，应该把所有的灯都关掉。

- We are also trying to make other changes. They include reducing the amount of trash we generate by recycling and composting, growing our own organic vegetables, and reusing and repurposing things that we would normally toss. 我们还试图进行其他改变，包括通过回收和堆肥来减少产生的垃圾量、种植有机蔬菜，以及重复使用和重新利用通常会被我们扔掉的那些东西。

- We can use reusable cloth shopping bags that are made from plant fibers. 我们可以使用由植物纤维制成的可重复使用的布质购物袋。

Exercise

1.	air pollution concentration	A.	森林覆盖率
2.	conserve natural habitats	B.	有机污染物
3.	endangered wildlife	C.	空气污染浓度
4.	eco-agriculture	D.	温室效应
5.	forest coverage	E.	保护生存环境
6.	greenhouse effect	F.	生态农业
7.	nature reserve	G.	濒危野生动物
8.	organic pollutant	H.	自然保护区
9.	over exploitation	I.	可生物降解塑料袋
10.	bio-degradable plastic bags	J.	过度利用

Section B   Picture-Related Description

Look at the following pictures and learn how to describe them.

 Conserving Electrical Power

In our tech-driven world, conserving electrical power is vital. Electricity fuels our lives, but as demand rises, we must take actions to save it. Simple steps like turning off lights and using energy-efficient appliances reduce consumption. Home improvements like insulation, LED lighting, and smart thermostats lower bills and carbon footprint. Governments and businesses should invest in renewable energy like solar and wind power to cut emissions and secure a green-energy future. Conserving electricity is our shared responsibility, leading to a greener world and reduced bills.

 Recycling

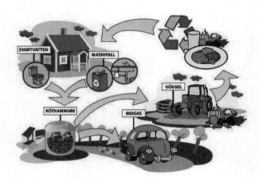

Recycling is the process of converting waste materials into new materials and objects. The recovery of energy from waste materials is often included in this concept. The recyclability of a material depends on its ability to reacquire the properties it has in its original state. It is an alternative to "conventional" waste disposal that can save materials and help lower greenhouse gas emissions. It can also prevent the waste of

potentially useful materials and reduce the consumption of fresh raw materials, reducing energy use, air pollution (from incineration), and water pollution (from landfilling).

 ## Renewable Energy

Renewable energy is collected from renewable resources that are naturally replenished on a human timescale. It includes sources such as sunlight, wind, rain, tides, waves, and geothermal heat. Renewable energy stands in contrast to fossil fuels, which are being used far more quickly than they are being replenished. Although most renewable energy sources are sustainable, some are not. For example, some biomass sources are considered unsustainable at current rates of exploitation. About 20% of global energy consumption is renewables, including almost 30% of electricity. About 8% of energy consumption is traditional biomass, but this is declining. Over 4% of energy consumption is heat energy from modern renewables, such as solar water heating, and over 6% is electricity.

 ## Low-Carbon Commuting

In our pursuit of a sustainable future, reconsidering our daily commute is paramount. Low-carbon commuting is key to curbing our carbon footprint and addressing climate change. Public transportation like trains, buses, and trams efficiently moves large numbers of people, reducing individual vehicles on the road and emissions. Carpooling and ridesharing maximize vehicle occupancy, further contributing to this objective. Cycling and walking are eco-friendly

options for short commutes, promoting personal health with zero carbon emissions. Electric vehicles, such as bikes and scooters, are increasingly popular due to their emission-free nature. Flexible work arrangements like telecommuting reduce the need for daily travel, while remote meetings and online collaboration tools cut business-related commuting.Low-carbon commuting not only reduces our environmental impact but also eases traffic congestion and enhances personal well-being. By embracing these practices, we pave the way for a cleaner, greener future.

 ## 5 Biodegradable and Recyclable Materials

As is the case for disposable cups, materials used are usually paper, plastic (including expanded polystyrene foam), or plastic-coated paper. Recycling rates are especially low for paper-based products, especially when soiled with (wet and/or oily) scraps due to diminished recycling quality. The waste problem is aggravated by the fact that most of the utilities themselves come in plastic and thus disposable packaging. Efforts are made to introduce biodegradable materials like sugarcane, bamboo, wheat straw, palm leaves, or various types of flours (rice, wheat, and sorghum). Nevertheless, non-biodegradable plastics often do not break down in landfill environments.

 ## 6 A Low-Carbon Diet

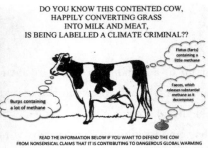

A low-carbon diet refers to making lifestyle choices related to food consumption to reduce resulting greenhouse gas emissions. Choosing a low-carbon diet is one facet of developing sustainable diets that increase the long-term sustainability of humanity. A low-carbon diet minimizes the emissions released from the production, packaging, processing, transport, preparation, and waste of food. Major tenets of a low-carbon diet include eating less industrial meat and dairy, eating less industrially produced food in general, eating foods grown locally and seasonally, eating less processed and packaged foods, and reducing waste from foods by proper portion sizes, recycling, or composting. By the way, vegetables are low-carbon compared with meats.

7　Water Conservation

　　Water conservation refers to using all the policies, strategies, and activities to sustainably manage the natural resource of fresh water, to protect the hydrosphere, and to meet the current and future human demand (thus avoiding water scarcity). The key activities to conserve water are as follows: any beneficial reduction in water loss, use, and waste of resources; avoiding any damage to water quality; and improving water management practices that reduce the use of or enhance the beneficial use of water. Technology solutions exist for households, commercial, and agricultural applications. Water conservation programs involved in social solutions are typically initiated at the local level, by either municipal water utilities or regional governments. Common strategies include public outreach campaigns, tiered water rates (charging progressively higher prices as water use increases), or restrictions on outdoor water use such as lawn watering and car washing.

8 Waste Sorting

Waste sorting is the process by which waste is separated into different elements. It can occur manually at the household. Waste can be collected through curbside collection schemes, or automatically separated in materials recovery facilities or mechanical biological treatment systems. Hand sorting was the first method used in the history of waste sorting. Waste segregation means dividing waste into dry and wet. Dry waste includes wood and related products, metals, and glass. Wet waste typically refers to organic waste usually generated by eating establishments and is heavy due to dampness. Waste segregation is different from waste sorting. Waste segregation is the grouping of waste into different categories. Each waste goes into its category at the point of dumping or collection, but sorting happens after dumping or collection. Waste segregation ensures pure and high-quality materials. Sorting on the other hand will end up producing impure materials with less quality.

Section C   Oral Practice

Part One

Look at the following pictures and have a talk with your partner using the prompting words.

 1   **Protecting the Earth**

Prompting words: use energy-efficient light bulbs; switch off the lights before going to sleep; take quicker showers; rechargeable batteries

 2   **Recycling**

Prompting words: second hand market; second hand goods; make full use of; an environmental-friendly action; recycling

3 Reusable Shopping Bags

Prompting words: stop using throw-away shopping bags; non-biodegradable materials; disposable plastic bags

 4 Recycling Old Clothes and Books

Prompting words: textbooks; recycle; environmental protection; reduce energy consuming; financial burden

 5 Solar Energy

Prompting words: renewable energy; device; solar roof water heaters; year round; storage; affordable price; tank

 6 Low-Carbon Travelling

Prompting words: choose to walk; ride a bike; take a bus/subway; shared bikes; solar power components; commuting; mobile apps; drop bikes anywhere

7 Energy Conserving at Home

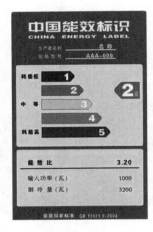

Prompting words: energy-efficient appliances; trade-in program; offer financial benefits and incentives to consumers; subsidies

8 Paperless Office

Prompting words: based on the Web; platform; the workflow management; take advantage of the Internet; improve the work efficiency

Part Two

Discuss the topic of sustainable living with your partner, and prepare a presentation.

1. **We have all been made aware of the warnings on the dangers associated with global warming, primarily caused by the burning of fossil fuels such as coal, oil, and gas. Simultaneously, the greenhouse effect has emerged as a significant environmental concern. When discussing your viewpoints on the danger of global warming with your partner, consider the following points:**
   - Factors contributing to the greenhouse effect and their mechanisms: Discuss the various factors that contribute to the greenhouse effect, such as carbon dioxide (CO_2), methane (CH_4), nitrous oxide (N_2O), and certain industrial gases. Explain how these gases trap heat in the Earth's atmosphere, leading to an increase in average global temperatures.
   - Differentiating between the greenhouse effect and global warming: Highlight the distinction between the greenhouse effect and global warming. Explain that the greenhouse effect is a natural process that helps regulate the Earth's temperature, whereas global warming refers to the long-term increase in average global temperatures caused by human activities, particularly the excessive emission of greenhouse gases.
   - The relationship between the greenhouse effect and global warming: Discuss the connection between the greenhouse effect and global warming, emphasizing that the greenhouse effect is the underlying mechanism that enables global warming to occur. Explain how the excessive accumulation of greenhouse gases intensifies the greenhouse effect, leading to an imbalance in the Earth's temperature and subsequent global warming.

2. **It is evident that many of the resources we depend on will eventually be depleted if we continue exploiting them at an ever-increasing rate. As college students, it is imperative for us to not only critically analyze these issues but also take actions within our capacity. When discussing sustainable resource utilization with your partner, consider the following questions:**
   - What is the significance of adopting a sustainable lifestyle? Have you ever contemplated the idea of embracing eco-friendly habits in your own life?

- How can we incorporate sustainable practices into our daily lives? Please share your personal experiences.
- In regard to the responsible development and utilization of non-renewable resources, what actions can we take to contribute to optimal sustainability?

3. **It is widely acknowledged that recycling plays a vital role in reducing environmental pollution by reducing the need for waste disposal facilities. When discussing the topic of reusing items with your partner, consider the following points:**
    - Highlight various consumer goods that can be reused instead of being discarded: Provide a list of examples that demonstrate how many consumer goods can be reused. Some examples include glass jars, plastic containers, shopping bags, clothing, furniture, and electronics.
    - Express your preference and reasoning when faced with purchasing regular batteries or investing in rechargeable batteries: Share your opinion on whether you would choose regular batteries at a lower price or invest in rechargeable batteries at a higher price when presented with the options by a shop assistant. Explain your decision-making process, considering the long-term benefits of rechargeable batteries, such as reduced waste, cost-effectiveness, and environmental impact.

4. **The rapid advancements in science and technology have greatly benefited our lives. When discussing technologies or inventions that align with the concept of a green lifestyle with your partner, such as shared bikes or paperless offices, consider the following points:**
    - Provide an example of an invention that contributes to a greener or more sustainable life: Share an example of an invention that has personally allowed you to live a greener or more sustainable life. For instance, you can talk about solar panels, electric vehicles, or smart home devices that optimize energy usage and reduce carbon footprint.
    - Explore innovative methods beyond new inventions: Highlight that aside from new inventions, there are also innovative ways to improve our life while being environmentally friendly. Mention the concept of shared bikes and inquire if your partner has ever used them. Prompt your partner to share his or her thought

on shared bikes, such as their convenience, impact on reducing car emissions, or potential challenges they may have faced.

5. **Since environmental issues have aroused close social attention, a lot of documentaries on environmental protection have come out. Introduce a few to the whole class and talk about which parts impress you the most. Use PowerPoint (PPT) slides during your presentation.**

Section D   Critical Thinking

Read the following passage that would help you better understand the related topics of this unit, and then discuss the questions with your partner.

An International Survey: Few Are Willing to Make Significant Lifestyle Changes for Environmental Protection

Citizens are alarmed by the climate crisis, but most believe they have already done more to preserve the planet than anyone else, including their government, and few are willing to make significant lifestyle changes, an international survey has found.

The survey found that 62% of people surveyed saw the climate crisis as the main environmental challenge the world was now facing, ahead of air pollution (39%), the impact of waste (38%), and new diseases (36%).

But when asked to rate their individual action against others' such as governments, businesses, and the media, people generally saw themselves as much more committed to the environment than others in their local community, or any institution.

About 36% rated themselves "highly committed" to preserving the planet, while only 21% felt the same was true of the media and 19% of the local government. A mere 18% felt their local community was equally committed, with national governments (17%) and big corporations (13%) seen as even less engaged.

Respondents were also lukewarm about doing more themselves, citing a wide range of reasons. Most (76%) of those surveyed said they would accept stricter environmental rules and regulations, but almost half (46%) felt that there was no real need for them to change their personal habits.

Only 51% said they would definitely take individual climate action, with 14% saying they would definitely not and 35% torn. People in Poland and Singapore (56%) were the most willing to act, and in Germany (44%) and the Netherlands (37%) the least.

The most common reasons given for not being willing to do more for the planet were "I feel proud of what I am currently doing" (74%), "There isn't agreement among experts on the best

solutions" (72%), and "I need more resources and equipment from public authorities" (69%).

Other reasons for not wanting to do more included "I can't afford to make those efforts" (60%), "I lack information and guidance on what to do" (55%), "I don't think individual efforts can really have an impact" (39%), "I believe environmental threats are overestimated" (35%), and "I don't have the headspace to think about it" (33%).

When asked which actions to preserve the planet should be prioritized, moreover, people attributed more importance to measures that had already been their established habits, required less individual effort, or for which they bore little direct responsibility.

About 57%, for example, said that reducing waste and increasing recycling were "very important". Other measures seen as priorities were reversing deforestation (54%), protecting endangered animal species (52%), building energy-efficient buildings (47%), and replacing fossil fuels with renewable energy (45%).

Respondents viewed measures likely to affect their own lifestyles, however, as significantly less important: Reducing people's energy consumption was seen as a priority by only 32%, while favoring public transport over cars (25%) and radically changing our agricultural model (24%) were similarly unpopular.

Only 23% felt that reducing plane travel and charging more for products that did not respect environmental norms were important to preserve the planet, while banning fossil fuel vehicles (22%) and reducing meat consumption (18%) and international trade (17%) were seen as even lower priorities.

"Citizens are undeniably concerned about the state of the planet, but these findings raise doubts regarding their level of commitment to preserving it," the study said. "Rather than translating into a greater willingness to change their habits, citizens' concerns are particularly focused on their negative assessment of governments' efforts."

Representative samples of more than 1,000 people were questioned in the U.S., the U.K., Spain, France, the Netherlands, Germany, Sweden, Poland, Singapore, and New Zealand.

People gave themselves the highest score for commitment everywhere except Sweden, while only in Singapore and New Zealand were national governments seen as highly engaged. The gulf between citizens' view of their own efforts (44%) and that of their government (16%) was the highest in the U.K.

Discussion

1. How might individuals' overestimation of their own environmental commitment compared with other entities (such as governments and businesses) hinder collective efforts to address the climate crisis?

2. In what ways do the reasons cited by individuals for unwilling to do more for the planet reflect cognitive biases or rationalizations, and how might addressing these barriers be key to fostering greater environmental protection action?

Unit 2
Tales of True Love

Learning Objectives

1. To acquire useful expressions about love;
2. To practice dialogs about love;
3. To present your ideas about love effectively;
4. To get more information about love.

Warm-up Questions

1 Do you believe in true love? Why or why not?

2 Have you ever fallen in love with someone?

3 What would your ideal spouse be like?

Section A Getting Ready to Speak

Part One

Read the following topic-related passages and answer the questions accordingly.

Dream of the Red Chamber

Written by litterateur Cao Xueqin in the Qing Dynasty, *Dream of the Red Chamber* is one of the four great classic novels in Chinese literature. The novel mainly centers on the love story of Jia Baoyu and Lin Daiyu.

Born to a Suzhou scholar-official, Lin Ruhai, and Lady Jia Min of the Rongguo House, Daiyu was raised by her parents in her family's mansion in Yangzhou, where she received an excellent education. When Daiyu was six, her mother died. Shortly after, she was summoned to the capital to live with her maternal grandmother, the powerful Jia Clan matriarch. She immediately bonded with Jia Baoyu, her maternal cousin, and with the many girl cousins in the house. Daiyu's father died a few years later, leaving her a complete orphan. Having a naturally weak constitution, Daiyu has been taking medicine and tonic from a very young age, and this resulted in her somewhat willowy build and ethereal beauty. Being willful, aloof, and oversensitive, she is shunned by other people around her, but her affectionate, naive, frank, and simple personality is such a match with that of Jia Baoyu, who finds her a congenial partner, claiming that he has seen her sometime somewhere. The two were drawn to each other and fell in love in secret; however, their love was thwarted by parental edicts. Baoyu's parents and Grandmother Jia had always believed that Jia Baoyu and his cousin Xue Baochai were a match made in heaven. Baochai, who was equally pretty but sensible, tolerant, and gentle, was preferred as the perfect wife for Baoyu. In the traditional wedding ceremony, a bride's face is covered during the entire process until the bride and her groom retire to their own chamber. They disguised Xue Baochai as Lin Daiyu and arranged a marriage between Baochai and Baoyu without the latter knowing the truth. An accidental leak of the preparation for Jia Baoyu's marriage with Xue Baochai by a maid struck Lin Daiyu down. Feeling betrayed, she asked Zijuan, her maid, to burn all the love letters Baoyu had written to her, and died in despair, with her tears literally running dry. Learning the truth about everything, Baoyu was like a walking ghost and later he became a monk at a temple.

Question 1: What is the background and upbringing of Lin Daiyu in *Dream of the Red Chamber*?

Question 2: How did the parental expectations play a role in the thwarting of the love between Jia Baoyu and Lin Daiyu in *Dream of the Red Chamber*?

A Ladder of Love

Over 50 years ago in a small village named Gaotan in southwestern China's Chongqing, a 19-year-old boy named Liu Guojiang fell in love with a 29-year-old widowed mother named Xu Chaoqing. At that time, it was socially unacceptable and immoral for a young man to love an older woman, let alone a widow with four young children. Criticism and gossip drove the couple to escape their village and start a new and arduous life high up in the mountains. They lived in an abandoned straw hut with no electricity, eating grass, herb roots, and other wild vegetables they found in the mountains. Liu made a kerosene lamp to light up their hut and they began to plant sweet potatoes and corn. To fend off storms and wild beasts, the couple built a sturdier shelter behind their hut. They also managed to collect mud and clay from a mountain pass and made their own tiles from a homemade kiln. In the second year of living in the mountain, Liu began to build a stairway in the mountains by hand so that his wife could ascend and descend the mountain easily. His work lasted for over 50 years and he chiseled more than 6,000 steps. It was not until 2001 that these steps came to the public attention when a research team on an expedition discovered them. The Ladder of Love has become well-known throughout China, inspiring television and movie adaptations as well as literary creations, even as Xu and Liu maintained their simple mountain life. Liu continued caring for his Ladder of Love until he died in 2007, at the age of 72. Xu passed away on October 30, 2012, and was buried together with her beloved husband in the same mountains where the two lived. The local government in the area has made efforts to maintain the love ladder and the place they lived as it was, so this pure love story can live forever.

Question 1: What challenges did Liu Guojiang and Xu Chaoqing face in their village, and how did they overcome societal criticism to pursue their love?

Question 2: How did Liu Guojiang demonstrate his love and dedication to Xu Chaoqing over the 50 years they spent together in the mountain?

Cowherd and Weaver Girl

Being one of the four great folktales of China, Cowherd (Niulang) and Weaver Girl (Zhinu) are widely known in China, which is a love story like Valentine and his lover. Niulang was an honest and kind cowherd who lived with his sole companion, an old ox. They depended on each other for survival. Niulang had been so kind to his old ox that the creature told him of a secret pond where the beautiful daughters of the Emperor of Heaven bathed. If Niulang stole one of their clothes, one of them would be unable to escape and become his wife. The girl whose clothes were stolen by Niulang happened to be Zhinu, the youngest and most beautiful daughter of the Emperor of Heaven. Niulang proposed marriage and Zhinu agreed, and the two got married. They lived a happy life on earth and gave birth to two lovely children.

When the Queen of Heaven found out the fact that her daughter had married a mortal, she was furious and immediately sent heavenly troops to catch Zhinu and bring her back. After he came home with his children, Niulang found her wife disappeared. The old ox, whom he had taken care of for many years, said he was too old and about to die. He told Niulang to wear his cowhide after he died so that he could go to heaven to find his wife. When Niulang was about to catch up with his wife, the Queen of Heaven waved her golden hairpin and created the Milky Way between them. Separated by the Milky Way, Niulang could only cry with his children for Zhinu on the opposite side. Moved by their love and devotion, countless magpies flocked together and created a bridge over the Milky Way, and Niulang and Zhinu got together on the magpie bridge. The Queen of Heaven was also moved and finally allowed the family to reunite on the magpie bridge on the seventh day of the seventh lunar month every year, which is called the Qixi Festival today, the Chinese Valentine's Day.

Question 1: What led to the separation of Niulang and Zhinu, and how did they attempt to reunite?

Question 2: How did Niulang and Zhinu finally reunite, and what special occasion in Chinese culture commemorates their love story?

Part Two

Act out the following dialogs with your partner. Change the role when necessary.

Jack:	Hi, Wang Ping.
Wang Ping:	Hi, Jack. I'm very glad that you've made it.
Jack:	Thank you for inviting me. I am really thrilled to have the opportunity to make moon cakes and experience Chinese traditional culture together with Chinese people.
Wang Ping:	We're also pleased to have you here. Let's look at what we have prepared. Here are three different types of stuffing, red bean paste, lotus paste, and five kernels. The dough has already been cut into small pieces. And there are the wooden molds with a carved pattern.
Jack:	Wow! You look very professional!
Wang Ping:	Not really! Come on, I'm going to show you how to make one.
Jack:	Nice!
Wang Ping:	Pick one small piece of dough and pat it flat into a round shape. Put in a small piece of stuffing and wrap it. Make sure it is well-wrapped by the dough. Put the dough with stuffing in the wooden mold and press it. You see, a beautifully-shaped moon cake!
Jack:	Wow, it looks so easy!
Wang Ping:	It is, actually.
Jack:	What is this pattern?
Wang Ping:	It's called Chang'e Benyue. It shows that Chang'e flew to the moon.
Jack:	Chang'e?
Wang Ping:	The love story of Chang'e and her husband Hou Yi is a popular fairy tale of the Mid-Autumn Festival. Once upon a time, 10 suns appeared in the sky. They looked like 10 fireballs, which scorched the entire Earth and people were dying. There was a sharpshooter named Hou Yi, Chang'e's husband, who attempted to help people shoot down the excess suns. Hou Yi shot down nine suns at one time and left only one. Because of his contribution to shooting down the suns and saving the world,

Queen Wang Mu gave Hou Yi a magic pill that could make him a god and become immortal. Hou Yi and Chang'e decided to share the magic pill on the Mid-Autumn Day when the light of the full moon shone on the Earth. However, one day an evil-minded man broke into Hou Yi's house and forced Chang'e to give him the pill. Chang'e worried that he would bring disasters to human beings after he got the magic, so she swallowed the pill. After swallowing the pill, Chang'e felt that her body became very light immediately. And she flew to the moon and became a goddess. Chang'e was accompanied by a jade rabbit on the moon every day. Ever since then, people started to celebrate the Mid-Autumn Day by appreciating the moon and eating moon cakes.

Jack: What a story!

Wang Ping: There are many fairy tales and stories in Chinese culture. You'll hear more stories.

Jack: I can't wait to find them out. Now, let me start to make moon cakes!

Wang Ping: Great!

Li Hai: Hello, Yueyue.

Yueyue: Hi! Glad to meet you here.

Li Hai: Me too.

Yueyue: What movie did you watch just now?

Li Hai: *Roman Holiday*, an old movie, but very classic. Have you watched it yet?

Yueyue: Yes. Who doesn't? It has always been popular among young people.

Li Hai: I like this story very much.

Yueyue: So do I. But I still feel sad that the two had to separate in the end. Why can't they stay together?

Li Hai: I guess that is because they both bear their responsibilities.

Yueyue: I used to think that a princess can do whatever she wants. She is born to be happy and enjoy her life.

Li Hai: Oh, no! Obligation is concomitant with privilege. A princess has enjoyed the privilege of the whole country. When it comes to the moment that her country needs her, she must shoulder her responsibility. Just like in ancient China, there used to be the policy of

cementing friendly relations with the peripheral countries through political marriage, for example, Princess Wen Cheng in the Tang Dynasty.

Yueyue: But things are different. That was a long time ago.

Li Hai: The times change but the rules don't. For Ann, her job was very clear. She was not only a princess but also a very good diplomat. She was beautiful, elegant, and well-educated, capable of speaking several languages. Her visit was to enhance trade relations between her motherland and other European countries. Being a royal family member, she was born to play that part.

Yueyue: But she didn't like it. She tried to escape.

Li Hai: Of course. She yearned for freedom. Since her life was arranged at the moment she was born, she never got a chance to enjoy freedom. Yet, she knew she could only escape for a while but not for her whole life. That's why she came back to resume her obligation.

Yueyue: I like happy endings. But maybe it is the best time for their departure because the two of them can leave a precious memory of each other.

Li Hai: Definitely. Love fades. The best way to keep it fresh is to end it.

Yueyue: Wow. I never thought of it that way! It sounds reasonable.

Xiaoxue: Tingting, what's up? Why are you sobbing?

Tingting: Nothing much. I am reading an article about the love story between Zhu Shenghao and Song Qingru. And I am greatly touched by their love.

Xiaoxue: Tell me about it. I'm all ears.

Tingting: Zhu and Song met at an event held by the River Poetry Society at Zhijiang University. Zhu was a senior and Song was a freshman then. They were both poetry lovers, and it was poetry that made two hearts grow fonder. The two began exchanging letters for 10 years until they got married in 1942. It's hard to imagine that Zhu, a quiet and reticent person could be so passionate and romantic in showing his love for Song. He wrote more than 500 love letters to her, addressing her in so many different ways and talking about his sadness, joy, frustration, satisfaction, ideas, and preferences. In one of his love letters to Song, he said: "I want to see the rain in the thatched pavilion, the ants by the rockery, the love of butterflies, the spider's web, the water, the boat, the cloud, the waterfall, and Song Qingru's sweet sleep."

Xiaoxue: Wow! How romantic! Did their love story have a happy ending?

Tingting: Sadly, no. Because Zhu was so dedicated to his translation work, his health became worse and worse. Two years after their marriage, Zhu died of tuberculosis at the age of 32, leaving Song devastated with grief.

Xiaoxue: What a pity! Just now you mentioned he was a translator. What did he translate?

Tingting: He succeeded in translating 31 plays of Shakespeare into Chinese during the Sino-Japanese War under extremely difficult circumstances, such as poverty, sickness, and shortage of reference materials. You know, some say that Zhu only did two things in his lifetime: One was to translate the complete works of William Shakespeare, and the other was to love Song Qingru.

Xiaoxue: That has a point. It is really a touching story. I feel like crying.

Tingting: Do you need some tissue?

Xiaoxue: Thanks!

Part Three

Read the following useful expressions and finish the matching exercise that follows.

- a match made in heaven 天作之合
- a solemn pledge of love 山盟海誓
- arranged marriage 包办婚姻
- ask someone out 邀某人约会
- be someone's one and only 成为某人的唯一挚爱
- bear and raise children 生儿育女
- blind date （由第三方安排的）男女初次约会
- break up / split up (with someone) 与某人分手
- bride 新娘
- cheat on someone 不忠实于（配偶或伴侣）
- chemistry 互相之间的吸引
- cohabitation 同居

- commuter marriage 通勤婚姻（两地分居）
- cyber love 网恋
- engagement 订婚
- fall head over heels in love 深陷情网，坠入爱河
- fancy someone 爱慕 / 爱恋某人
- fiancé 未婚夫
- fiancée 未婚妻
- flash wedding 闪婚
- groom 新郎
- have a crush on someone 暗恋某人
- have an affair 婚外情
- in-laws 姻亲
- interracial marriage 跨种族婚姻
- long-distance relationship 异地恋
- love at first sight 一见钟情
- love someone with all of one's heart and soul 全身心地爱某人
- marriage of convenience （出于实际需要、金钱或政治原因的）权宜婚姻
- matchmaker 媒人
- monogamy 一夫一妻制
- online dating 网络交友
- Platonic love 柏拉图式爱情
- propose to someone / propose marriage 向某人求婚
- puppy love 少男少女不成熟的恋爱
- Qixi Festival 七夕节
- romance 爱情故事；风流韵事
- shotgun marriage 奉子成婚
- soul mate 灵魂伴侣
- speed dating 速配约会

- spouse 配偶
- the orders of parents and the words of matchmakers 父母之命，媒妁之言
- tie the knot 喜结连理
- trial marriage 试婚
- unrequited love 单相思
- Valentine's Day 情人节
- wedding anniversary 结婚纪念日
- wedding ceremony 结婚典礼
- whirlwind romance 闪电式恋爱
- Have you ever fallen in love with someone? 你曾经爱上过某人吗？
- Is there true love in this world? 世界上有真爱吗？
- How long have you been dating him? 你和他约会多久了？
- When did you fall out of love with me? 你从什么时候开始不爱我了？
- Does love last forever? 爱是永恒的吗？
- Do you believe in love at first sight? 你相信一见钟情吗？
- Where were you when he popped the question? 他在哪里向你求婚的？
- A heart that loves is always young. 有爱的心永远年轻。
- Brief is life, but love is long. 生命虽短，爱却绵长。
- Love is not a matter of counting the days; it's making the days count. 爱不是数着日子生活，而是让每天都变得有意义。
- I love you not because of who you are, but because of who I am when I am with you. 我爱你，不是因为你是谁，而是因为在你面前我可以是谁。
- There is plenty of fish in the sea. 天涯何处无芳草。
- The worst way to miss someone is to be sitting right beside them knowing you can't have them. 失去某人最糟糕的莫过于，他近在身旁，却犹如远在天边。
- To the world you may be one person, but to one person you may be the world. 对世界而言，你是一个人；但对于某个人来说，你是一个世界。
- To love and to be loved is the greatest happiness of existence. 爱人和被人爱

是人生最大的幸福。

- It is better to remain single than settle for someone incompatible. 宁可单身也不随随便便嫁人。

- Every man is a poet when he is in love. 每个恋爱中的人都是诗人。

- First love is only a little foolishness and a lot of curiosity. 初恋就是一点点笨拙外加许许多多好奇。

- A good marriage brings you happiness; only a bad marriage can make you become a philosopher. 美好的婚姻会给你带来幸福，不幸的婚姻则可使你成为哲学家。

- Men marry because they are tired, women because they are curious; both are disappointed. 男人因疲倦而结婚，女人因好奇而结婚，最终两人都大失所望。

Exercise

1.	a match made in heaven	A.	闪婚
2.	arranged marriage	B.	灵魂伴侣
3.	love at first sight	C.	不忠实于（配偶或伴侣）
4.	online dating	D.	（由第三方安排的）男女初次约会
5.	long-distance relationship	E.	天作之合
6.	soul mate	F.	一见钟情
7.	monogamy	G.	包办婚姻
8.	flash wedding	H.	网络交友
9.	blind date	I.	一夫一妻制
10.	cheat on someone	J.	异地恋

Section B   Picture-Related Description

Look at the following pictures and learn how to describe them.

1   The Butterfly Lover

The Chinese fairy tale, the Butterfly Lover, tells a love tragedy between Liang Shanbo and Zhu Yingtai in the Eastern Jin Dynasty.

At that time, girls were not allowed to go to public schools. Zhu Yingtai disguised herself as a man to go to Songshan Academy. There, she met Liang Shanbo and fell in love with him.

School ended and they went home together. On the way back, Zhu promised Liang a marriage with her sister. By saying so, she obviously meant herself. When Liang realized that Zhu was a girl and she made a promise to marry him, he was thrilled. But unfortunately, Zhu's family had already betrothed her to Ma Wencai, a son of a local high official. No one could change her father's decision.

Heartbroken and desperate, Liang soon fell terribly sick and died in his sadness. Zhu heard the news and decided to die for love after him. On her wedding day, Zhu paid a visit to Liang's tomb and she cried so desperately and prayed the heaven to open up the tomb. Her prayer was answered and the tomb split open. She hopped in and then the tomb soon closed. The couple turned into a pair of butterflies and would never be separated again.

2 *Song of Everlasting Regret*

Song of Everlasting Regret, written by Bai Juyi, depicts the tragic love stories between Emperor Tang Xuanzong and Yang Yuhuan.

Yang Yuhuan was very beautiful and she was listed as one of the four ancient beauties of China. Her beauty was so irresistible that Tang Xuanzong, her father-in-law, took her roughly as a concubine against the father-son bond and morality. Tang's indulgence in enjoyment and

neglect of the state affairs finally led to An Lushan's rebellion in 755. Disgruntled officers and soldiers called for Tang Xuanzong to execute Yang Yuhuan. Because of her tragic ending, Tang Xuanzong was remorseful for the rest of his life.

3 *Romance of the West Chamber*

Romance of the West Chamber, written by the playwright Wang Shifu in the Yuan Dynasty, tells the love story between Zhang Sheng, a scholar, and Cui Yingying, the daughter of a former chief minister.

Zhang Sheng was a poor scholar. One day, he paid a visit to a temple, where he met Cui Yingying and was attracted by her charm. Unfortunately, a local bandit was drawn by Cui's

beauty as well, hoping to take Cui as his consort. He dispatched his men to besiege them on the way to the temple. In order to protect her daughter, Cui's mother promised to marry her daughter to whoever saves her. With the help of his friends, Zhang managed to drive away the bandit. But Cui's mother backed out and broke off their engagement. It was Cui's maid, Hong Niang, who had helped them go through hardships and get married finally.

Zhuo Wenjun and Sima Xiangru

The famous love story of Zhuo Wenjun and Sima Xiangru in the Han Dynasty was recorded by *Phoenix Seeking His Mate* (*Feng Qiu Huang*), a piece of Guzheng music.

Sima Xiangru was a renowned poet of his time, while Zhuo Wenjun was the widowed daughter of Zhuo Wangsun in Sichuan Province. Sima was invited to a party held by Zhuo's father at his house where he played a song by Guqin (Chinese zither). When Zhuo was listening from the next room, a sudden gust of wind rolled the curtain and they fell in love with each other at first sight. Against her father's will, Zhuo ran away with Sima and started to sell liquor to support the family since Sima was a poor man. In the end, her father forgave them and gave his approval to their marriage.

 The Peacocks Flying to the Southeast

The Peacocks Flying to the Southeast was written by a Chinese poet Xie Lingyun. Being the first song narrative poem in Chinese literary history, the poem tells a love tragedy in the Eastern Han Dynasty.

Jiao Zhongqing, son of a declining official family, married Liu Lanzhi, daughter of a poor family. Though the couple loved each other deeply, Liu was maltreated by her mother-in-law. She couldn't bear it finally and left her husband. But it was not the end of her tragedy. She went back to her family and was forced to marry her elder brother. Unwilling to remarry, Liu drowned herself in a lake. Hearing her death, Jiao would like to die together with his wife and hanged himself on a tree.

6   Marriage of the Fairy Princess

Marriage of the Fairy Princess is a widely known love story in China that tells the legend of Dong Yong and the Seventh Fairy.

The legend happened in the Eastern Han Dynasty (25–220). Dong Yong had to sell himself into slavery because his father died and left him a mountain of debt. Moved by his kindness, honesty, and filial piety, the Seventh Fairy descended to earth to marry him without

the knowledge of her father, the king of heaven. Dong Yong worked in the field, while the Seventh Fairy weaved cloth. They worked so hard that the couple managed to buy back Dong's freedom. When the Jade Emperor finally found out about his daughter's escape, she was asked to return to Heaven. Otherwise, Dong Yong would be killed. The Seventh Fairy had no choice but to leave. A year later, their son was sent to Dong Yong and the couple never got a chance to see each other again.

7   Jane Eyre

Jane Eyre was a plain, but intelligent orphan, living with unpleasant relatives. At the age of 18, Jane accepted a teaching post at Thornfield Hall. She fell in love with her employer, Edward Rochester, despite the clear difference in their social status.

They agreed to be married. However, on their wedding day, Jane learned that Rochester had a wife, an insane woman, who was concealed away in the upper chambers of Thornfield. Heartbroken, Jane made the agonizing decision to leave.

Eventually, Jane inherited a substantial fortune and decided to return to Thornfield. She discovered Mrs. Rochester died in

the conflagration. Jane happily married Rochester, who had gone blind in the fire.

8 *Legend of the White Snake*

Legend of the White Snake is one of the most popular fairy tales that has spread out among folks for centuries in China.

The White Snake, a snake spirit, transformed into a beautiful young lady and looked for Xu Xian who had saved her life in the human world. Luckily, she met him and fell in love with him. Since she was not a real human, their marriage was unallowable in the human world.

Having been made to drink realgar liquor, the White Snake lost her power and couldn't help but reveal her snake body. Xu died of shock and the White Snake brought him back to life. Fahai, a Buddhist monk in Jinshan Temple, took Xu as a hostage and suppressed the White Snake under the Leifeng Pagoda. The couple didn't get the chance to see each other again until years later when their son grew up and managed to free his mother from the pagoda. The whole family reunited and stayed together ever-after.

Section C　Oral Practice

Part One

Look at the following pictures and have a talk with your partner using the prompting words.

1 Du Liniang and Liu Mengmei

Prompting words: Kunqu Opera; the Peony Pavilion; *Book of Songs*; freedom of love; resurrection

2 Meng Jiangnu

Prompting words: Emperor Qin Shi Huang; the Great Wall; Shanhai Pass; hardship; collapse

3 Xiang Yu and Yu Ji

Prompting words: King of West Chu; slit one's throat; suicide; the Wu River; besiege

4 Chang'e Flying to the Moon

Prompting words: a valiant archer named Hou Yi; an elixir of immortality; float up to the sky; heartbroken; the Mid-Autumn Festival

5 *Titanic*

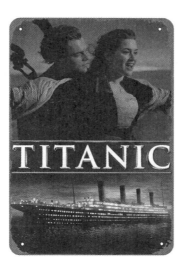

Prompting words: a penniless artist named Jack; Rose; loveless engagement; fall in love; sacrifice; survive the shipwreck

6 Li Qingzhao and Zhao Mingcheng

Prompting words: poet; have a crush on each other; dedicate; epigraphy; compile; sorrow

7   **Wu Sangui and Chen Yuanyuan**

Prompting words: fall in love; at the first sight; concubine; Shanhai Pass; the Qing army; surrender

8   **Yuan Zhen and Wei Cong**

Prompting words: die young; lost; not ready to move on; miss; loyalty; cherish the memory of

Part Two

Discuss the following questions with your partner to talk about love.

1. **Talk about love.**
   - What is love?
   - Do you believe there are different types of love? If yes, what are they?
   - Do you believe in love at the first sight? Why or why not?

2. **Talk about relationships.**
   - What qualities of a partner are important for you?
   - Describe your ideal date.
   - Would you go on a blind date?
   - Do you think it's possible to find love on the Internet?

3. **Talk about marriage.**
   - Is it better to be single or married?
   - What do you think the secret to a happy marriage is?
   - Do you think marriage changes people? In what ways?

4. **In modern society, it's common for couples to live together before getting married. Talk about this phenomenon.**
   - What are the pros and cons of living together before getting married?
   - Suppose your boyfriend or girlfriend asks you to live with him or her, would you agree? Why or why not?

5. **China's divorce rate has been climbing. Between 1987 and 2020, the number of divorce registrations in the country surged from 580,000 to 3.73 million, with the divorce rate rising from 0.5% in 1987 to 3.4% in 2019.**
   - Do you know anyone who has gotten divorced? Do you know the reasons of their divorce?
   - Why has the divorce rate increased over the years?

Section D Critical Thinking

Read the following passage that would help you better understand the related topics of this unit, and then discuss the questions with your partner.

Lin Juemin's Farewell Letter to His Wife

Yi Ying my dearest,

Please listen. I am writing this to say my last goodbye to you. I write this as one who lives in this world, but by the time you read this, I would have become a shade in the underworld. Ink and tears flow in equal measure as I write. Time and again I have had to put my pen away, unable to finish, but I am afraid you would not understand why I would be so cruel as to leave you behind, that I would be uncaring of your sadness at my parting. And so I persist.

I love you dearly, to the end, and this love we have is what gives me the courage to face death. Since I have met you, I have often wished that all those who love would find their fulfillment. But everywhere I look, the world is immersed in blood and turmoil. How many families can truly say they are happy? My country's sadness is mine to bear. I am not like the great sages who can hold themselves aloof, unmoved by the travails of the world. It is said: "Decency is to take care of the old as you would your own parents, to take care of the young as you would your own children." As my heart is filled with my love for you, so it is that same heart that yearns for broader happiness, so that all who love can find love. That is where I get my courage to leave you, to depart the world ahead of you. If I am leaving you uncared for, please understand, even in your tears of sadness, that I do this for every one of us, and be glad that the sacrifice we make of our love and your well-being is for each, and every one of us, in the hope of bringing lasting happiness to our country. Do not feel so sad.

Do you remember, about four or five years ago, I once said. If we were to die, I wished that you would go first. You were angry when you first heard it until I had a chance to explain. And even as you did not agree, you were unable to contradict me. What I meant was that I knew you would not have been able to bear the sadness of my death if I was to die first. My death would have left you in a cruel agony. I would rather that it was me who would bear the sadness of our separation in death. Alas, it is I who will have to go first!

I truly will never forget our time together. I remember our house in the back street, how we entered through the hallway, passed the front and back parlors into the smaller parlor after a few turns, and the little room there where we have spent so much time together as husband and wife. Remember in the third or fourth months after we were married. It was mid-month. We looked out the window together, to see the village under moonlight and shadows, partly obscured by the bare branches of the plum trees. Side by side, hand in hand, softly we talked. Was there anything we did not talk about? Were there any words of love we did not say to each other? Through my tears I remember. And I remember six, seven years ago, when I suddenly left mysteriously without telling you where. You told me tearfully afterward: "From now on, you must tell me whenever you have to travel far away. I will follow you wherever you go." I promised you then that I would. About ten days ago when I came home, I had wanted to tell you about this journey far away, but when I faced you I could not find words. And you were pregnant. I was afraid you could not bear it. If I have been taking refuge in drinks these last few days, it is to contain my sadness.

I truly want to live out my life together with you, but when I look around and see what can end our lives—natural calamities can kill us, thieves and robbers can kill us, the upheaval in the breaking up of China can kill us, corrupt, despotic officials who abuse us can kill us. In today's China, death strikes us at any time, any place. When that time comes for us to die, should I watch you die with my open eyes, or should you watch me die? Can we do that? Even if we survive, what is to prevent us from being torn apart? And even if we look for each other until our bones turn into fossils, how many couples forced apart have ever gotten back together in all of history? It is worse than death. We are fortunate to be alive and together today, but how many were there who had wished to live and yet perished? How many couples who had wished to be together and yet were forcefully separated? Countless. How many of us in our time, who love as we do can endure any of this? This is why I have made the decision to lay down my life, even if it means leaving you. I will have no regrets. And if the country is not put to right, there will be others like me who will come after to carry on. Yi Sun is five now; he will be a grown man soon. Raise him well, let him be like me. I think that the life in your belly is a girl. It will look like you, and I am glad. If it is a boy, teach him about my aspirations, so that even with my death, there will be two others of the same mind. I should be so happy, so very happy. You will be poor with me gone. Poverty is not a great hardship for a life lived simply.

I have no more words. If I should hear your cries from afar when I am in the underworld, I will cry together with you. I do not believe in ghosts, but now I hope ghosts do exist. Some people talk of hearts being joined. I hope there are such things, so that after my death, my spirit will follow close to you, always, and you will never be sad for the lack of a companion.

I had not revealed to you my ideals for our country. It is my fault. If I had told you, you would have been worried every day. I do not fear death, but I cannot bear your worrying about me. I love you, to the end, and I am afraid I have not been able to arrange everything properly for you. How fortunate we are that you met me. How unfortunate we are to have been born in today's China. How fortunate I am to have you. How unfortunate to have been born in today's China. A man cannot tend only to his interest. What can I do? So much love, but such a small handkerchief. So many words from the heart left unsaid, but I know you can glean the rest. I won't be able to see you again. I know you won't be able to forget me. Would you see me in your dreams? I am tumultuous!

Written in the year Xinhai, the twenty-sixth of the third month, in the fourth watch of the night.

All our female relatives can read. Please ask them for help if anything is unclear. I want you to really understand.

Discussion

1. What do you think Lin Juemin valued most in his family relationships based on the letter?
2. What challenges do you think Lin Juemin faced in balancing his personal aspirations with family expectations?

Unit 3
Friendship

Learning Objectives

1. To acquire useful expressions about friendship;
2. To practice dialogs about friendship;
3. To present your ideas about friendship effectively;
4. To get more information about friendship.

Warm-up Questions

① What's real friendship?
② What could friendship bring to you?
③ What kind of person deserves real friendship? Why or why not?

Section A   Getting Ready to Speak

Part One

Read the following topic-related passages and answer the questions accordingly.

 Yu Boya and Zhong Ziqi

During the Warring States Period, there was a person named Yu Boya, who played the Guzheng very well. One day, when he was playing the Guzheng on a mountain, there came a firewood man called Zhong Ziqi. As soon as Yu played the Guzheng, Zhong said, "The sound is like Mount Tai." Yu was surprised because he was just trying to show the mountains. Yu wondered whether Zhong could perceive the musical theme changes if he shifted the musical theme to water. After hearing the new sound, Zhong said, "The sound is like a river." No matter what Yu played, Zhong could understand what the music conveyed. So the two persons became good friends. But a few months later, Zhong died. Yu was so sad about losing his friend that he broke his Guzheng and vowed not to play it any more. The story later formed the idiom "high mountains and running water" and a commonly used word in daily life, i.e. "bosom friend".

Question 1: Why did Yu Boya and Zhong Ziqi become good friends?
Question 2: What happened to Yu Boya after Zhong Ziqi died?

Lin Xiangru and Lian Po

During the Warring States Period, Lin Xiangru was promoted to Shangqing because of his great achievements, ranking above Lian Po. Harboring a grudge against him, Lian tried to get back at him. After Lin knew it, he avoided Lian everywhere. Once Lian's and Lin's carriages met on a narrow road, Lin, as the higher-ranking minister, normally had the right of passage; however, he turned and backed out of the street in order to let Lian pass. The attendants were very dissatisfied with Lin's tolerant behavior. Lin explained, "The feud between me and Lian Po is a personal one; but I am in charge of the nation's government, and he the nation's security. I can't let my personal life ruin that of the kingdom." When Lian finally heard of this, all his jealousy turned into shame. Deciding to apologize to Lin, he strapped brambles to his bare back and walked to Lin's house, begging for his forgiveness. Lin forgave him, and from then on, they became good friends. The alliance between the chief minister and the general kept Zhao peaceful for years.

Question 1: Why did Lin Xiangru avoid Lian Po after being promoted to Shangqing?

Question 2: How did Lian Po apologize to Lin Xiangru?

Friendship

Friends play an important part in our lives, and we may take friendship for granted, but often don't clearly understand how we make friends. While we get on well with a number of people, we usually become friends with only a very few, for example, the average number among students is about six per person. In all the cases of friendly relationships, two people like one another and enjoy being together, but beyond that, the degree of intimacy between them and the reasons for their shared interest vary enormously. As we get to know people, we take into account things like age, race, economic condition, social position, and intelligence. Although these factors are not of prime importance, it is more difficult to get on with people when there is a marked difference in age and background.

Question 1: What is the average number of friends a student usually has according to the text?

Question 2: How do factors like age, race, economic condition, social position, and intelligence affect our relationships with people, despite not being of prime importance?

Part Two

Act out the following dialogs with your partner. Change the role when necessary.

Ryan: Hey! You look depressed. What's up?

James: Well, nothing big. I found out one of my friends blocked me. I wonder why some friendships endure and others slip way quickly. What do you think makes a friendship strong enough to endure?

Ryan: Oh, to me, a strong friendship is built on the foundation of trust and mutual respect. No friendship can go well without it.

James: Right, But what should we do when we grow up and change? Does friendship need any adjustments?

Ryan: Absolutely! Good friends will make some adjustments and support each other despite differences.

James: What do you think about conflicts in friendship?

Ryan: Well, conflicts can also lead to the end of friendships. When conflicts happen, putting yourself in other's shoes is a good way to deal with the problems. In this way, the friendship can endure storms , and even become stronger.

James: It makes sense. And sometimes, we can rarely predict at the outset which friendships will last forever.

Ryan: Exactly! Most friendships do enrich us, like a chapter in our life story, teaching us something new and shaping who we are.

James: Yes, I'm feeling much better now. Time for lunch. Let's have lunch together.

Ryan: Sounds great!

A: What's your view on friendship?

B: Well, I think friendship is one of the most important things in life.

C: Oh, I feel the same way. But some people don't know the real meaning of friendship.

A: So, what's the real meaning of it?

B: A friend in need is a friend indeed. Don't you think so?

C: Yes, I do.

A: Then, what's your opinion?

B: I think it is only partly true. As far as I'm concerned, a real friend should also be able to share your happy moments without feeling jealous.

C: You're right. I've been promoted recently, but one of my good friends just pretended to be happy about my promotion. I could feel that he was actually very unhappy.

A: It just goes to show that he is not your true friend.

C: Maybe.

B: I haven't finished my definition of friendship.

A: Well, tell us, we're all ears.

B: Honesty is also an essential part of any friendship. We should learn to accept our friends for who they are.

A: You've got a point there.

C: Will you make female friends after you get married?

A: Although family life is fulfilling, it isn't enough. I can get tremendous satisfaction from my friends, male and female, married and single. I will not marry a boy who is against making male friends.

B: I have the same idea.

C: You know, in China, many men will not have women friends after they get married.

A & B: Why?

C: There might be two reasons. First, their wives will not be happy if their husbands continue their friendship with female friends. Second, probably, there is no true friendship between a man and a woman.

A: Oh, but I hope we are friends forever.

B & C: Yeah, so do we.

Jack: What kind of qualities do you look for in your friends?

Joan: I like to make friends with people who are open and friendly. These people are usually active and fun to be with.

Jack: Sure. But sometimes those who are not open and active can become very good friends.

Joan: Of course! So that's why a person always has different kinds of friends in his life.

Jack: Yes. I like to make friends with those whom I can get along well with.

Joan: Sure! Who will make friends with those he cannot get on well?

Jack: Oh, don't get me wrong. I'm just saying that maybe you don't have much in common, yet you feel very comfortable when you are with each other. That's a great feeling.

Joan: I agree. But generally, I prefer to make friends with those who share similar interests with me. We can do a lot of things together and it's great fun. I love spending time with my friends.

Jack: That certainly is good. But I think the more important thing about friendship is that you can share happiness and sorrow, you can always help each other when in trouble, and you can cheer each other up when disheartened.

Joan: Yes, that is true. So I think being a good friend means you have to be supportive, willing to help, honest, trustworthy, and a good listener. These qualities are important in maintaining good friendships.

Jack: Absolutely! Everyone needs friends. Friendship plays an important role in our life.

Joan: I completely agree with you.

Part Three

Read the following useful expressions and finish the matching exercise that follows.

- active 思想活跃的
- a stable personality and high sense of responsibility 个性稳重、责任感强
- bright and aggressive 反应快、有进取心的
- considerate 体贴的
- creative and innovative 有首创和革新精神的
- elegant 举止优雅的
- energetic and fashionable 精力旺盛和新潮的
- generous 慷慨的
- fair weather friends 不能共患难的朋友
- independent 独立的
- maintain friendships into adulthood 将友谊维持到成年
- mature and honest 思想成熟且为人诚实的
- out-going 外向的
- positive 积极的
- shy and introverted 害羞且内向的
- seeds of friendship 友谊的种子
- self-motivated and strong interpersonal skills 上进心强，并具有良好的人际交往能力
- sincere 真诚的
- strengthen friendship 增进友谊
- strong determination to succeed 有获得成功的坚定决心
- sworn friends 莫逆之交
- A bosom friend afar brings distant land near. 海内存知己，天涯若比邻。
- A brother may not be a friend, but a friend will always be a brother. 兄弟未必

是朋友，而朋友总是兄弟。

- A friend in need is a friend indeed. 患难见真情。
- A true friend is known in the day of adversity. 疾风知劲草，患难见真情。
- A life without a friend is a life without a sun. 人生在世无朋友，犹如生活无太阳。
- A friend without faults will never be found. 没有缺点的朋友是永远找不到的。
- A real friend never gets in your way, unless you happen to be on the way down. 真正的朋友决不会挡住你的去路，除非你在走下坡路。
- A good book is the best of friends, the same today and forever. 好书如挚友，情谊永不渝。
- A man knows his companion in a long journey and a little inn. 路遥知马力，日久见人心。
- A hedge between keeps friendship green. 君子之交淡如水。
- Be slow in choosing a friend, slower in changing. 选择朋友要谨慎，换朋友更要谨慎。
- Better lose a jest than a friend. 宁失一谑，不失一友。
- Choose an author as you choose a friend. 选书如择友。
- Friendship lasts forever. 友谊地久天长。
- Friendship is the greatest pleasure in life. 友谊是人生最大的快乐。
- Familiar paths and old friends are the best. 熟路好遵循，老友最可珍。
- Friendship is love with understanding. 友谊是爱加上谅解。
- Friendship multiplies joys and divides grieves. 友谊可以增添欢乐，可以分担忧愁。
- Friends may meet, but mountains never greet. 朋友可相逢，高山永分离。
- Friendship is like money, easier made than kept. 友谊如金钱一般，容易得到却不易保持。
- Friendship is like a plant of slow growth. 友谊是像植物一样慢慢建立起来的。
- Friendship is to be strengthened by truth and devotion. 友谊要以真实和忠诚来巩固。

- Friends are like fiddle strings; they must not be screwed too tight. 朋友像琴弦，不能拧太紧。

- If you would be loved, love and be lovable. 想被人爱，就要爱别人，并让自己可爱。

- Without a friend, the world is a wilderness. 没有朋友，世界就等于一片荒野。

- When all else is lost, the future still remains. 就是失去了一切别的，也还有未来。

- Some components of a thriving friendship are honesty, naturalness, thoughtfulness, and some common interests. 确保友谊常青的要素是：诚实、朴实自然、体贴和某些共同兴趣。

- They were both waiting for the other one to break the ice. 两人都在等另一方先开口。

- Trust not the praise of a friend, nor the contempt of an enemy. 不要信赖朋友的赞扬，也不要把仇敌的轻蔑放在心上。

- To preserve a friend, three things are required: to honor him present, praise him absent, and assist him in his necessities. 维持友谊需要三点：当面尊重他，背后赞扬他，以及需要时帮助他。

- Without words, in friendship, all thoughts, all desires, all expectations, are silent joy and sharing. 在友谊里不用言语，一切的思想、愿望和希冀，都在无声的欢乐中发生而共享了。

- You flatter me immensely. 你过奖啦。

- "Friendship is the purest love. It is the highest form of love where nothing is expected in return." 友谊是最纯净的爱，它是最高形式的爱，无须期待回报。

Exercise

1.	A bosom friend afar brings distant land near.	**A.**	友谊是爱加上谅解。
2.	A friend in need is a friend indeed.	**B.**	友谊要以真实和忠诚来巩固。
3.	Friendship is love with understanding.	**C.**	海内存知己，天涯若比邻。
4.	Without a friend, the world is a wilderness.	**D.**	患难见真情。
5.	strengthen friendship	**E.**	害羞且内向的
6.	seeds of friendship	**F.**	莫逆之交
7.	Friendship is to be strengthened by truth and devotion.	**G.**	没有朋友，世界就等于一片荒野。
8.	shy and introverted	**H.**	思想成熟且为人诚实的
9.	mature and honest	**I.**	增进友谊
10.	sworn friends	**J.**	友谊的种子

Section B Picture-Related Description

Look at the following pictures and learn how to describe them.

1 True Friendship

During the Eastern Han Dynasty, a scholar named Gong Shamu lived in seclusion in Donglaishan. In order to raise funds for his study, he put on coarse clothes and worked as rice-pounding worker in Lord Wu's home of Chenliu County. Appreciating his extraordinary eloquence, Lord Wu made friends with him and funded him to continue his study. Later, Gong Shamu became an accomplished and just official.

2 Liu Zongyuan and Liu Yuxi

In 793 AD, Liu Zongyuan and Liu Yuxi were both successful in the imperial examination when Liu Zongyuan was 20 years old and Liu Yuxi was 21. The two ambitious young men worked together in Jingzhaofu, and forged a profound friendship based on shared ideals and pursuits. Having ups and downs in the officialdom, they always stood up for each other during times of exile. Their friendship gradually deepened through mutual assistance in their life, and they became lifelong close friends.

3 Li Bai and Du Fu

Li Bai and Du Fu were two outstanding poets of the Tang Dynasty in China, and their friendship is cherished as an unforgettable episode in the history of ancient Chinese literature. In approximately 744 AD, the two poets met in Luoyang, where Li Bai was already a renowned figure, while Du Fu had yet to attain fame. Later they enjoyed themselves while exploring the mountains and rivers, discussing poetry. Despite an age difference of eleven years, they swiftly forged a profound bond due to their shared literary pursuits and passion for poetry.

4 "Presented to Wang Lun"

Li Bai on board, ready to push off, suddenly heard the tramping and singing on the bank

Peach Blossom Pond a thousand feet deep is shallower than the love of Wang Lun who sees me off.

"Presented to Wang Lun" is a farewell poem written by the renowned poet Li Bai in the Tang Dynasty during his visit to the Peach Blossom Pond in Jing County, which is located in the southern Anhui Province of China now. The poem captures the heartfelt farewell scene between Li Bai and his local friend Wang Lun and also becomes a masterpiece of Chinese poetry.

5   Guan Zhong and Bao Shuya

"Guan Bao" refers to Guan Zhong and Bao Shuya, Chinese politicians in the Spring and Autumn Period, who were good friends. Guan was poor and Bao was relatively rich, but they knew and trusted each other. The profound friendship between Guan and Bao has become a good story handed down from generation to generation in China. In China, people often use "Guan Bao Zhi Jiao" to describe the close and trusting relationship between them.

6   Friendship Between Old and Young People

When Mi Heng made friends with Kong Rong, Mi was 20 years younger than Kong, who was already 50 years old. Kong valued Mi's talent so that he was willing to be his best friend in spite of the difference in age. Later, "Wang Nian Zhi Jiao", a Chinese idiom, was used to refer to making friends regardless of age.

7 Childhood Friend

Li Bai, the most famous poet in the Tang Dynasty, has a poem describing children happily enjoying each other. The poem says, "The boy came on a bamboo-horse, wandered around the bed with green plums in hand; grew up together in Chang-gan-li, the two little friends had no suspicion between them." It means children usually share good feelings and rarely have fights.

8 Guan Ning and Hua Xin

In the Eastern Han Dynasty, Guan Ning and Hua Xin were classmates and friends. One day, they were weeding in the garden and found a piece of gold in the field. Guan regarded the gold as a tile and waved his hoe, while Hua picked up the gold and put it aside. Once again, the two were reading at the same table. When some dignitaries passed by, Guan was undisturbed, but Hua went out to watch with an envious look. Guan thought that Hua and he were not really like-minded friends, so he split the straw mat they shared. Since then, he didn't regard Hua as his friend anymore.

 # Section C   Oral Practice

Part One

Look at the following pictures and have a talk with your partner using the prompting words.

 Taking Oath in the Peach Garden

Prompting words: peach blossom; peach wood; swear; loyalty; take oath

 Bosom Friend

Prompting words: appreciate; artistic conception; Guzheng; musical instrument; theme

3   **Kong Rong and Mi Heng**

Prompting words: a big age gap; impressive; cross-generation; mutual affection; intimate

 4   **Chen Zhong and Lei Yi**

Prompting words: interests; courageous; for the sake of others; wisdom and virtue; honorable

5   Jiao Ai and Bo Tao

Prompting words: share happiness and sorrow; sacrifice; noble deeds; hand down; profound friendship

6   Yuan Bo and Ju Qing

Prompting words: honesty; truly great friends; profound friendship; agree on a date; keep the promise

7 **Lianpo and Lin Xiangru**

Promoting words: a thorny stick; kneel down; apologize; profound friendship; forgive

 8 **Guan Zhong and Bao Shuya**

Prompting words: close, trusting relationship; respect; assistance; profound friendship

Part Two

Discuss the following questions with your partner to talk about your friends.

1. **Introduce your friends to your partner and your talk should include the following questions:**
   - Who are your best friends?
   - Show the pictures to your partner, and tell them the feeling while you are there with your friends.
   - Try to explain why you are good friends.

2. **Happiness is always an attractive topic for your friends. Talk about the happy moments with your friends and your talk should include the following questions:**
   - Do you have any happy moments with your friends?
   - Share these stories with your partner and make them want to know more details.

3. **Take a minute to think about a moving story with your friends, something you see as important in your life, and your talk should include the following questions:**
   - What did you do in the story?
   - What did your friend do in the story?
   - Why did the story move you?

4. **Discuss the following questions with your partner and your talk should include the following question:**
   - What do you think are the most important qualities for friends to have?

5. **After all these preparations, design a presentation and introduce your friends to your class. You can use PPT slides in your presentation.**

Section D   Critical Thinking

Read the following passage that would help you better understand the related topics of this unit, and then discuss the questions with your partner.

On Friendship

And a youth said, speak to us of friendship.

And he answered, saying:

Your friend is your needs answered.

He is your field which you sow with love and reap with thanksgiving.

And he is your board and your fireside.

For you come to him with your hunger, and you seek him for peace.

When your friend speaks his mind you fear not the "nay" in your own mind, nor do you withhold the "ay".

And when he is silent your heart ceases not to listen to his heart;

For without words, in friendship, all thoughts, all desires, and all expectations are born and shared, with joy that is unclaimed.

When you part from your friend, you grieve not;

For that which you love most in him may be clearer in his absence, as the mountain to the climber is clearer from the plain.

And let there be no purpose in friendship save the deepening of the spirit.

For love that seeks aught but the disclosure of its own mystery is not love but a net cast forth: and only the unprofitable is caught.

Discussion

1. What do you believe is the most important quality in friendship? Why?
2. Do you believe disappointment and setbacks are inevitable in friendship? Why? How would you deal with such setbacks? What inspiration did this passage give you?

Unit 4
Studying Abroad

Learning Objectives

1. To acquire useful expressions about studying abroad;
2. To practice dialogs about the related topics;
3. To present your ideas about studying abroad effectively;
4. To get more information about studying abroad.

Warm-up Questions

① Do you have the intention to study abroad? Why or why not?
② Which country will you choose to study in?
③ Which university and which specialty do you prefer?

Section A   Getting Ready to Speak

Part One

Read the following topic-related passages and answer the questions accordingly.

Pros and Cons While Studying Abroad

Nowadays, with globalization making the world more interconnected, the trend of pursuing higher education has been on the rise. It is important to know the benefits and downsides before you make that final decision.

Firstly, in terms of education, it is important for the youth to improve themselves with the great help of the first-rate education outside. Besides, they would also benefit from the language-rich atmosphere in foreign countries. However, the study reveals that more than 70% of overseas students in the U.K. face serious language barriers in their first half year, which may lead to misunderstandings and other issues.

Furthermore, from an economic perspective, a diploma from a reputable university is a must for an ideal profession, which is equivalent to a good salary; in addition, it brings about qualified social welfare as insurance for the rest of your life. Despite this, the expensive and unreasonable tuition costs prevent countless students from pursuing higher education.

Lastly, from a cultural perspective, the multi-cultural society enables people to broaden their horizons day by day. Naturally, it would promote international connections among countries. Then, one will have a full awareness of globalization. Nevertheless, not every student or individual can bear the cultural shock when he or she is abroad. In addition, discrimination gives rise to some

psychological issues at the same time, such as loneliness and homesickness.

All in all, my point of view on this issue is manifest. And studying abroad has more advantages than disadvantages.

Question 1: What are the pros of studying abroad according to the text?

Question 2: What are the cons of studying abroad according to the text?

What Can You Study in China?

When you study in China, you can enrich your academic studies while experiencing the unique rural and metropolitan beauty of the country. China is a vast country with a rich culture and history, a thriving economy, and a large population. This creates plenty of opportunities to learn both in and out of the classroom. You can gain a new, Chinese perspective on your studies. For instance, you can learn how business, education, or language studies are handled, or develop a better understanding of Chinese culture and history. Then, when you're not in the classroom, you can explore the vast country's outdoor offerings, distinctive food, and historical sites.

Studying in China doesn't mean you have to take a break from your academic studies. On the contrary, you can continue to earn valuable credits while simultaneously gaining a new perspective on your study field. Many courses are offered in English, helping make sure you won't miss a step.

Some of the following concentrations might be especially interested in pursuing classes in China. Be aware that these are not the only options available and that courses may differ by programs.

Education Courses

Students majoring in education might be interested in learning to teach English as a second language (ESL) while studying in China. Many education programs cover different ESL methods and techniques through a combination of coursework and hands-on learning. You can not only develop your teaching knowledge by taking courses yourself, but also have the chance to teach English to your Chinese classmates, immediately testing out new teaching methods and techniques in a real-world setting.

Language Courses

Living and studying in China might be a great opportunity to study Mandarin or Cantonese. Depending on where you choose to study in China, you can take intensive courses in either of the above-mentioned languages. Besides, the whole country can become your classroom. Stepping outside your door, you can have a great chance to test your Chinese knowledge. Go ahead and try to place your usual lunch order in Mandarin or Cantonese!

Business Courses

With many of the programs located in cultural and financial epicenters, it's no wonder that business students might be interested in taking courses in China. Business courses can illustrate how Chinese companies are structured and function, or provide a unique perspective on global economics or business in Asia. By studying in Beijing or Shanghai, students may even have the chance to visit industry leaders' headquarters as part of their program.

Question 1: What are the places to learn languages when you study in China?

Question 2: What can you learn when you study in China?

My Views on Studying Abroad

Studying abroad, to some people, sounds like a dream. The opportunity to travel and experience a new way of life can be great. To others, however, studying abroad may appear like a complete nightmare—being far away from your family in a strange culture can be very scary. Actually, studying abroad is only a good idea if it is something you may enjoy, otherwise you will not be able to have a positive experience. But if you do decide to study abroad, it is important to know the advantages and disadvantages before you finally make the decision.

Studying abroad can teach you invaluable life lessons about what you do enjoy and you can learn great independence skills. Some of these things may sound trivial, but it may be the first time you have had to budget for yourself, cook and clean for yourself, do the shopping, and so on. You will also get a great sense of freedom, meaning you will have to learn how to discipline yourself. It is all too easy to forget that one of the goals you go abroad is to study, and you must focus a large part of your time on your academic studies and not solely on your new-found freedom and social life of course! Furthermore, once you come to writing your curriculum vitae, being able to enclose international exposure is a definite selling point. It shows potential employers that you are independent, dedicated, and hard-working as well as aware of global and international issues. In addition, as discussed above, you will learn a certain subject from a different cultural perspective, meaning you have extensive knowledge on this subject that other people may not have.

Of course, if you study abroad, you will leave behind your friends and your family for a period of time. This can be very hard, particularly if you have never been away from home for any great length of time. You will also need to interrupt all activities you are involved in at home, such as sports or voluntary activities. Another con is that you do not exactly know what to expect, and you can be in for a disappointment. Being independent in a foreign country can be very hard. Furthermore, your accommodation might not be up to standards, or you may have very annoying neighbors or roommates. These may be things that are harder to sort out while abroad, especially if you are struggling with the language.

It is also possible that you find you cannot settle in the foreign culture. Different cultures have different habits, and you may find it very hard to learn how to live with these, or how to live without certain habits that come so naturally to your own culture.

It is important for you to carefully weigh up the pros and cons of studying abroad and ensure that you have contingency plans in place for every con you may come across. Once you know the pros and cons of studying abroad and you decide to go, stand by your decision and believe in yourself.

Question 1: Would you prefer to study abroad? Why or why not?

Question 2: What else do you expect to get besides knowledge when studying abroad?

Part Two

Act out the following dialogs with your partner. Change the role when necessary.

A: What do you think of studying abroad?

B: I think it's a great idea. Studying abroad will offer you plenty of new opportunities. Are you planning to go abroad?

A: Yes, I hope to. I am studying for my IELTS right now.

B: Which country do you want to go to?

A: I'd like to study in the U.K., but it's quite expensive.

B: Have you applied for any schools there?

A: Yes, I received a conditional offer from Oxford University a few days ago.

B: Congratulations! That's excellent news! What do you have to do to get an unconditional offer?

A: I have to get an IELTS score of 7.5 overall. Do you think I can do that?

B: Of course, if you study hard, you can make it. Have you received any other offers?

A: I was also accepted into Yale University and Sydney University.

B: If you're worried about money, the cost of living is the lowest in Australia. However, if you go to Oxford University, you'll probably be able to get any job you want in the future.

A: I just can't decide which one to go. It's not an easy decision to make.

B: If I were you, I'd apply for some scholarships and grants before I decide. Whatever you do, I know you'll succeed.

A: Guess what came in the mail today?

B: What?

A: My acceptance letter to Yale!

B: Wow! Congratulations! When do classes start?

A: The freshman orientation is the last week of August, but I want to go two weeks before that to get settled in.

B: You're so lucky! Do you have to do many things before you leave?

A: Yes. I'll be very busy! I have to pack, get a visa, and buy a plane ticket. But first, I want to register for class.

B: When can you do that?

A: Well, they sent me their prospectus, so I can start now. Do you want to help me decide what class to take?

B: Sure. What can you choose from?

A: Well, I have to take the entire fundamental courses, plus a few from my major.

B: What is your major?

A: I hope to major in English Literature, but the admissions counselor told me that many people often change their majors in their first year, so I'll wait and see.

B: What are the fundamental courses?

A: In order to graduate, every student must take a specific number of classes in history, math, English, philosophy, science, and art.

B: Interesting. That's very different from the Chinese education system.

A: Yes, it is. It's also very different from the British education system.

B: Really?

A: Oh, sure. In Britain, students don't have to take the fundamental courses.

B: Why not?

A: Maybe because they think they have known everything already! Ha ha.

A: Can I ask you some questions?

B: Yes, please.

A: What do you intend to do in the U.K.?

B: I'd like to further my study and pursue my Master's degree.

A: Well, I can see you're going to take courses in English literature, which is not very popular in China but pretty hard for Chinese students. Are you confident that you can handle it very well?

B: Yes, I am. I'm really interested in English literature. I have studied it for four years in university and I'm one of the top five students in my class.

A: Can I have a look at your letter of acceptance?

B: Sure. Here is the original copy.

A: How do you pay your tuition fees and other expenses during your stay in the U.K.?

B: My parents will support me. Here are the affidavits of support from them, a bank statement of their financial status, and some of their bank deposit receipts.

A: Are you coming back to China after you've got your degree?

B: Of course. As an English major, it won't be easy for me to get a job in the U.K. But in China, I'll have more opportunities. I hope I can make contributions to my homeland in the future.

A: OK. Your passport will be ready in a week.

B: Thank you very much.

Part Three

Read the following useful expressions and finish the matching exercise that follows.

- admission 录取
- advisor 指导教师
- application 申请
- applicant 申请人
- culture shock 文化冲击
- destination 目的地
- embassy 大使馆
- form 表格
- financial aid 助学金
- host family 接受留学生的家庭
- homestay / family stay / host stay 寄宿家庭
- interview 面试
- IELTS 雅思
- insurance 保险
- letter of acceptance 接受函
- passport 护照
- prestige 声望
- recommendation 推荐
- resume 简历
- scholarship 奖学金
- transcript 学生成绩单
- TOEFL 托福
- tuition fees and other expenses 学费和其他花费
- university accommodation 学校宿舍

- visa 签证
- a bank statement of one's financial status and some bank deposit receipts 财务状况银行声明和一些存款收据
- a comprehensive and national key university 一所综合性全国重点大学
- apply for a school 向一所学校申请
- apply for a student visa 申请学生签证
- apply for financial aid 申请助学金
- be accepted/admitted to a school 被一所学校录取
- choose electives 选择选修课
- defer enrollment 推迟入学
- get a copy of one's transcripts 获得某人成绩单的复印件
- fill in the application form 填写申请表格
- register for class 报名 / 注册上课
- weigh up the pros and cons of studying abroad 权衡出国留学的利与弊
- I think it's a great idea. Studying abroad will offer you plenty of new opportunities. 我觉得这是个很好的想法。出国留学能为你提供很多新机会。
- I received a conditional offer from Oxford University a few days ago. 几天前，我收到了牛津大学的有条件录取通知书。
- I've been so stressed these days. 我这几天压力很大。
- I'm looking for some materials for a paper I'm writing, and I'm not quite sure where to look. 我在找一些写论文的材料，但不太清楚去哪里找。
- I'm not sure which hall the register will assign to us. During the reading period, I'm sure they will have posted the exam location list. Check then. 我不太清楚教务处会把我们安排在哪里考试。等上课以后，我相信他们会把考试地点张贴出来，到那时再查一下。
- I can't catch up with the English teacher very well. 我跟不上英语老师的课。
- Do you know what studying abroad programs will be available this year? 你知道今年有哪些出国学习项目可以申请吗？

- Hello, this is the admissions office. Can I help you? 你好，这里是招生办公室，有什么可以为您效劳？

- Do you have any catalogs from U.S. universities? 你们有美国大学的概况手册吗？

- In order to reduce culture shock, it would be beneficial for the students to obtain specific training both in the foreign language and in cross-cultural competence before they go abroad. 为了减少文化冲击，让学生出国前获得外语强化训练和跨文化培训是有好处的。

- Get down to business if you wouldn't like to flunk out. 如果你不想被学校开除，就赶紧做正事吧！

- Here's the course description guide. 这是一份课程说明。

- Hi, I'm calling about your continuing education program. 你好，我打电话是想咨询一下你们学校继续教育课程的有关情况。

- I'm pretty busy. I have to pick up a lot of credits this year. 我很忙。我今年要修很多学分。

- Right. We might as well be nervous about something we know, instead of something we don't know. 是啊，与其对未知的事情感到紧张，还不如为已知的事情紧张。

- Studying abroad can widen our vision and broaden our minds. 出国留学能开阔我们的视野和思维。

- Studying abroad is not suitable for everyone because of the high costs and fees. 由于高昂的花费和学费，并不是人人都适合出国留学。

- What do you think of studying abroad? 你觉得出国留学怎么样？

- What are you going to do for your year abroad? 你在国外的这一年打算做什么？

- What's your schedule like this year? 你今年的课程安排怎么样？

- What do I do with it? 它对我有什么作用？

- Where are you planning to transfer to? 你打算转到哪个专业？

- You should do anything you can to improve your English. 你应该尽一切可能来提高自己的英语水平。

Exercise

1.	host family	A.	学生成绩单
2.	embassy	B.	保险
3.	destination	C.	目的地
4.	insurance	D.	大使馆
5.	transcript	E.	接受留学生的家庭
6.	resume	F.	声望
7.	financial aid	G.	奖学金
8.	scholarship	H.	助学金
9.	prestige	I.	简历
10.	advisor	J.	指导教师

Section B   Picture-Related Description

Look at the following pictures and learn how to describe them.

 1 **Peking University**

Peking University is a cradle of top-quality and creative students, a major source of cutting-edge science and knowledge innovation, and a key bridge for international exchange. It has six faculties, namely Humanities, Social Sciences, Economics and Management, Science, Information Technology and Engineering, as well as Health Science. It consists of 55 schools and departments, 60 research entities, and ten affiliated hospitals.

Peking University stands at the forefront of global academic research and fosters talents that lead the world to the future. With undergraduate education as its cornerstone, it integrates general and professional education, in an effort to invigorate quality and efficient undergraduate education. It explores different approaches for educating different postgraduate students, and establishes a postgraduate education system for developing first-rate leaders.

 2 **Tsinghua University**

The campus of Tsinghua University is situated in northwest Beijing and surrounded by a number of historical sites. Since China opened up to the world in 1978, Tsinghua University has developed at a breathtaking pace into a comprehensive research university. At present, the university has 21 schools and 59 departments with faculties in science, engineering, humanities, law, medicine, history, philosophy, economics, management, education, and art.

With the motto of "Self-discipline and Social Commitment" and the spirit of "Actions Speak Louder than Words", Tsinghua University is dedicated to the well-being of Chinese society and world development. As one of China's most prestigious and influential universities, it is committed to cultivating global citizens who will thrive in today's world and become tomorrow's leaders.

 Columbia University

Columbia is a private graduate school in Manhattan, New York. It is one of the world's most important centers of research and at the same time a distinctive and distinguished learning environment for undergraduates and graduate students in many scholarly and professional fields. It seeks to attract a diverse and international faculty, staff, and student body, to support research and teaching on global

issues, and to create academic relationships with many countries and regions. It expects all areas of the University to advance knowledge and learning at the highest level and to convey the products of its efforts to the world.

 Stanford University

Located between San Francisco and San Jose in the heart of Silicon Valley, Stanford University is recognized as one of the world's leading research and teaching institutions. Stanford was founded almost 150 years ago on a bedrock of societal purpose. Its mission is to contribute to the world by educating students for lives of leadership and contribution with integrity; advancing

fundamental knowledge and cultivating creativity; leading in pioneering research for effective clinical therapies; and accelerating solutions and amplifying their impact.

Stanford offers students broad and deep academic programs across seven schools and multiple fields—including the arts and humanities, natural and social sciences, engineering, sustainability, medicine, law, education, and business.

5   Experiencing an Exotic Life

When you study in China, you can enrich your academic studies while experiencing the unique rural and metropolitan beauty of the country. China is a vast country with a rich culture and history, a thriving economy, and a large population. This creates plenty of opportunities for you to learn both in and out of the classroom. You can gain a new, Chinese perspective on your studies. For instance, you can learn how business, education, or language studies are handled, or develop a better understanding of Chinese culture and history. Then, when you're not in the classroom, you could explore the vast country's outdoor offerings, distinctive food, and historical sites.

 6 Challenges of Studying Abroad

Nowadays, with globalization making the world more interconnected, the trend of accepting higher education has been on the rise. Many students consider studying abroad, and here are some of the challenges they may confront. The first one is being exposed to a totally exotic environment. People who study abroad will be open to everything new and strange. On a social level, they may also meet

a diverse range of counterparts. Sometimes it is not easy to become the ice-breaker. Another challenge may come from their family: The overseas students will be more likely to be homesick, especially for those who are in their first year. Besides, we shall not forget the obstacles of culture and language. Even if they can understand every single word, they will still fail to grasp the true meaning. Despite all these challenges, there are still a lot of people choosing to study abroad, because great challenges always come along with great opportunities.

 7 Tips for Studying Abroad

It is important to ensure that you have contingency plans in place for every con you may come across when studying abroad. It is also important to seriously study the country you are planning to study in, because laws and ideas can be very different abroad. Many countries still discriminate against certain groups of population, such as women or homosexuals. Before you go, you need to have everything in

place. You also need a place to stay and potentially a visa and inoculations. Make sure you meet all the requirements of your chosen country, including financial issues such as the need for a bank account. Once you decide to go for it, stand by your decision and believe in yourself.

8 Keeping Cultural Awareness in Mind

When you travel, live, and study abroad, you should keep cultural awareness in mind. What's cultural awareness? It refers to one's understanding of the differences between oneself and people from other countries or other backgrounds, especially differences in attitudes and values. Cultural awareness is the foundation of communication and it involves the ability to stand back from ourselves and become aware of our cultural values, beliefs, and perceptions. Why do you do things in that way? How do we see the world? Why do we react in that particular way? Cultural awareness becomes central when we have to interact with people from other cultures. People see, interpret, and evaluate things in different ways. What is considered an appropriate behavior in one culture might be inappropriate in another one. Misunderstandings often arise when we use our meanings to make sense of our reality. That is why cultural awareness may prove to be very valuable.

 # Section C Oral Practice

Part One

Look at the following pictures and have a talk with your partner using the prompting words.

 1 **Fudan University**

   Prompting words: established; Fudan University; Bachelor's degree; doctoral degree; academic disciplines

 2 **Shanghai Jiaotong University**

   Prompting words: high scientific research level; technological innovation level; cultural heritage; internationalized; world-class university

3 Massachusetts Institute of Technology

Prompting words: private graduate school; world-class faculty and facilities; creativity; innovation and collaboration; launch its "Open Course Ware" program

4 Harvard University

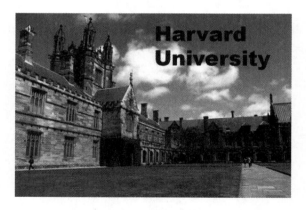

Prompting words: leading; institution; private graduate school; academic pedigree; executive education

5   Preparing for Studying Abroad

Promoting words: apply for; GPA; English proficiency test; accommodation; study visa

6   Tips for Making Friends When You Study Abroad

Promoting words: experiencing a new culture; open-minded; meet people from every corner of the globe; mutual; respect

7 Tips for Studying Abroad

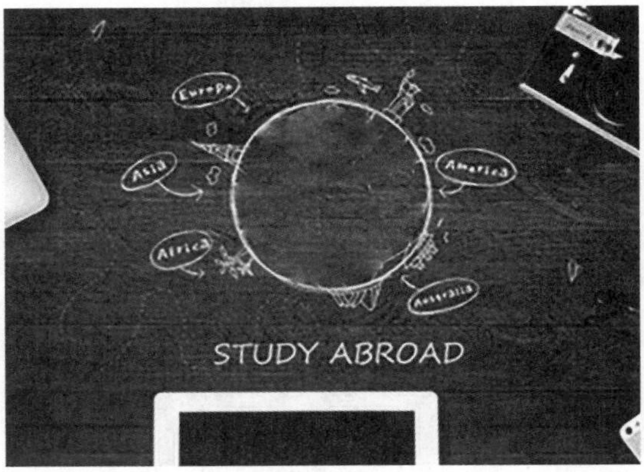

Promoting words: cultural concerns; prerequisite; accommodation; visa; ethnic

8 Studying in Shanghai

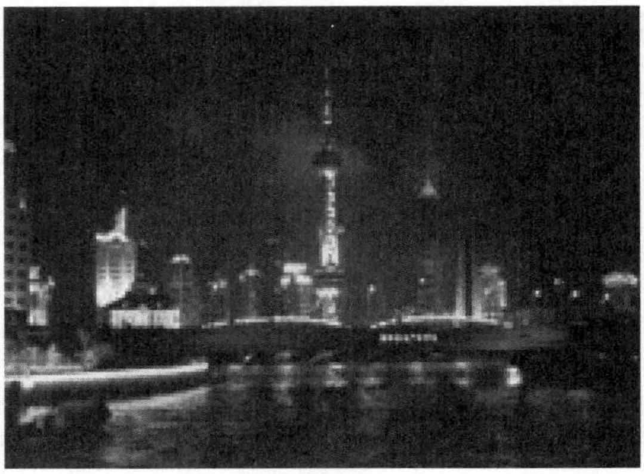

Promoting words: Yangtze River Delta; cosmopolitan; unique heritage; booming economy; commercial and financial center

Part Two

Discuss the following questions with your partner to talk about your university.

1. Everyone is somehow proud of his/her university. When someone talks about his/her university with friends, he/she always begins with its history, surroundings, and specialties. Introduce your university to your friends in details, and your talk should include the following questions:
   - What is the history of your university?
   - Is there any famous scenic spot in your university?
   - Is there any famous and delicious food in your university?
   - Is there any famous person from your university?

2. You want to invite your friends to visit your university. As a host, you should guide them to travel in your university, and your talk should include the following points:
   - A brief overview of the campus layout, highlighting some of the unique features or attractions on campus, such as beautiful gardens, modern buildings, or famous artworks, mentioning any specific events, activities, or facilities available for students.

3. After all these preparations, design a presentation to present your university to your class as a tour guide. You can use PPT slides in your presentation.

4. You're incredibly excited to study abroad and experience a new culture. You will not only embark on an adventure you'll never forget, but also learn a lot and broaden your horizons in the process. Try to describe in detail about your future university based on the following questions:
   - Which university would you like to study in?
   - Which major or subject will you study?
   - Are there any well-known professors in the university?
   - Are you staying with a host family? How will you feel if you stay with them?

5. When you're in a foreign country, immerse yourself in it. Try to speak the language as much as possible, make friends, and watch TV shows on the local channels. You can consider the following questions:

- What benefits can you get by immersing yourself in a new environment?
- What additional benefits can you get by watching local TV shows?
- What other ways can you find to adapt to the new life and environment?

Section D Critical Thinking

Read the following passage that would help you better understand the related topics of this unit, and then discuss the questions.

Reasons to Study Abroad

Here's our list of 25 reasons to study abroad. And for those of you who have already studied abroad, let us know if you can think of any more good reasons to study abroad and whether you agree with the list so far!

1. It'll look good on your CV. Experience of living internationally goes well with employers, showing you have experience of dealing with people from different cultures, plus a higher level of adaptability. If you can explore a new country and pick up skills to gain a decent graduate job, then it's pretty good going.

2. Brush up on your language skills. Remember the foreign languages you learned in school? No, me neither. Refresh them by studying abroad; you might be surprised at how much you remember. Taking extra language classes when you're out there can also be a great way to meet new people.

3. Living in a foreign country is completely different to a holiday. You'll actually get to experience your place of study in the long term, picking up local knowledge such as where sells the best coffee, what tourist traps to avoid, and how to get the most out of the city.

4. Meet a diverse range of people. Your exposure to many different types of people will not only help you develop your communication skills, but also give you a more in-depth knowledge of others, particularly those from different cultures.

5. Make lifelong friends. You may not love every single person you meet, but chances are that you'll meet at least one lifelong friend (if you're good at keeping in touch). A shared international study experience is a great way to bond with your fellow students.

6. Discover new and exciting foods. Get more paella/poutine/pierogi/schnitzel/shawarma/chimichanga/katsudon/bobotie/baklava in your life.

7. Study and learn differently. Often those studying abroad will experience a completely new way of teaching. This can be daunting, but it will also open your mind to new ways of learning.

8. Gain independence. Studying and living abroad requires you to be independent, without the safety of your home comforts. You will look at this as an exciting new challenge (rather than something terrifying).

9. Learn self-reliance. Moving abroad is the ultimate test of self-reliance. When you move back, you'll likely rely on others less and you'll take more responsibility for yourself.

10. You'll gain a greater knowledge of different cultures. Cultural sensitivity isn't just a quality that politicians may be accused of lacking; it's also something you can develop while studying abroad!

11. See your own culture through a new lens. It's easy to accept your own culture as absolute, but living in another country can help inform your point of view on your home culture, allowing you to develop your own views rather than simply accepting those defined by where you happen to come from.

12. Learn more about yourself. Throwing yourself into a completely new environment will help you figure out what you're good at, as well as what you're not so good at. These are things that can then be built on during your studying-abroad experience.

13. Become an adult. Speed up the transition from teenager to adult by leaping into the unknown. You'll have to fend for yourself, buy your own meals, and wash your own clothes, but it'll all be worth it.

14. Gain life experience. One of the ultimate reasons to study abroad is to gain life experience. You'll learn how to organize your life and condense it into one suitcase, handle unforeseen situations, and be independent and self-sufficient.

15. Be spontaneous and adventurous. When you're thousands of miles away from home, spontaneity and adventure are your best friends. Open your mind up to new experiences and sights and the fun will come your way.

16. You learn to appreciate the smaller things more. Studying abroad usually means you have even fewer possessions than the average student, and being that much further from home can really make you miss those familiar comforts you'd taken for granted. Welcome to a new-found appreciation of everything from your parents' cooking to having more than two pairs of shoes to choose from.

17. Gain a global mindset. Whether it's in work, study, or play, you'll be able to use your new

global mindset to back up arguments, inform your beliefs, and steer your future.

18. Get the perks of international student discounts. Student discounts are always fun but 100 times more so when you're shopping in a new store with funny-looking money!

19. It's an unforgettable experience. Even if your friends back home get bored of hearing about it, your studying-abroad experience will stay with you long after it's over.

20. You'll appreciate your home and family more. Any memories of parental arguments or sibling rivalry will pale in comparison to your memories of how amazing they are. Likewise, they'll have time to forget about all your less attractive attributes too...When you get back, these relationships will look so much stronger!

21. International student funding is becoming more common. Studying abroad doesn't have to leave you penniless, as more and more institutions and governmental bodies are offering dedicated scholarships for international students.

22. Take advantage of lower tuition fees. This, of course, depends on where you study abroad, but if you choose a location in many parts of continental Europe, Asia, and Latin America, you'll find it's possible to study at a highly reputed university without getting into too much debt.

23. Use your spare time to explore. In between lectures and lab sessions, studying abroad should leave you with plenty of time to explore. Whether you're one for visiting iconic landmarks, trying new foods, or bartering at local markets, there's always bound to be a better way of spending your time than scrolling through Facebook!

24. Increase your international job prospects. While you can always go home at the end of your time as an international student, many choose to stay put and apply for a working visa. Even if you return home or decide to seek work elsewhere, the international experience provided by studying abroad is likely to be looked on favorably by employers.

25. Variety is the spice of life. It might be something your dad says when opting for a different flavor of crisps at the supermarket, but it's true; change, variety, and new experiences are what make life worth living. Mix it up a bit: Study abroad!

Discussion

1. Can you list some reasons not to study abroad?
2. Do you agree to all the reasons listed in the passage? Present your arguments if you disagree.

Unit 5
Maker Movement

Learning Objectives

1. To acquire useful expressions used in oral tasks on the Maker Movement;
2. To practice expressions for the related topic on the Maker Movement;
3. To present your ideas effectively about the Maker Movement;
4. To get more information about makers and what they are doing now in China.

Warm-up Questions

1. Do you know anyone who is a maker?
2. How do makers and their actions change our life?
3. What's the significance of the Maker Movement in China?

Section A Getting Ready to Speak

Part One

Read the following topic-related passages and answer the questions according to the passages.

A Surprise Gift and a Promise

Several young students of a maker association at Tsinghua University were in for a surprise from Premier Li Keqiang on May 4, China's Youth Day. In a letter, the Premier encourages the young makers to be adventurous and innovative, and start their own business.

Derived from the West, the word "maker"—which primarily means people who are enthusiastic about entrepreneurship and innovation—has gradually become a hot topic in China. The Premier explicitly pointed out in his Government Work Report in March that public entrepreneurship and innovation are "two engines" to drive the Chinese economy, which is experiencing downward pressure.

"I hope college students will work hard to seek the truth instead of being content with what they have already known. I hope they will lay a solid academic foundation for their research. College students should not only learn from books but also from practice. The most important part of public entrepreneurship and innovation is to encourage people's creativity, especially young people whose willingness and determination lead to a prosperous and vigorous society and country," the Premier said in the letter.

As the Premier also noted in the letter, the government will push forward more preferential policies for makers, and young makers feel there is a new era around the corner. For the Tsinghua students, the letter is a gift. But for all makers, it is a promise they have been waiting for.

Questions

1. Why does the author say the letter is a gift?
2. Why does the author say the letter is a promise?

Maker Faire Showcases Students' Inventions

Riddhiman Gupta, a sixth-grader at Shanghai Community International School, has invented a convenient mask vending machine. Made from recycled paper boxes and with easy gear, the light and cheap device can be installed at local subway stations, office buildings, shopping malls, and other public places where masks are compulsory due to COVID-19 measures.

His invention was one of the innovative exhibits at the Maker Faire Shanghai 2021, a carnival gathering local tech enthusiasts, craft workers, educators, hobbyists, engineers, science clubs, authors, artists, and students. About 15,000 visitors, mainly local parents and children as well as expatriates, attended the annual maker faire. The event features more than 60 interactive and engaging booths such as 3D printing, robot-wars, science experiments, coding, pottery, wood-working, and many other maker/STEAM (science, technology, engineering, and math) education activities.

Started in 2006 in the San Francisco Bay Area, the movement has since spread to countries all over the world with more than 200 maker faires in places such as Tokyo, Rome, Shenzhen, Taipei, Seoul, Paris, Berlin, and Barcelona. "The event aims to create a platform for individuals and small companies to showcase their innovative ideas," said Praveen Rao, co-founder of Maker Faire Shanghai. "Children are expected to be inspired by various scientific experiments and innovation designs."

Ladies Who Tech in Action: Beauty Tech

Ladies Who Tech was started by women who are in the STEM industries and believe in challenging the status quo by encouraging more women to assist and discover their potential in STEM. We want to raise awareness of the lack of women in the STEM industries and help companies have more diversity.

The human race of all genders and all ages has been pursuing perfection in beauty from ancient times to the modern era. When beauty personalization is combined with digital technologies, the results can be game-changing.

In the context of science innovation, how would digital transformation, advanced tech, and biotech help us explore the most personalized and best solutions to our beauty needs?

This coming April 29, Ladies Who Tech Chengdu invites experts from Microsoft, Shiseido Beauty Innovation Hub, 23mofang, and Le Glamour Suisse Sarl to share and explore the topic of beauty personalization: How technology is creating new opportunities for personalized beauty experiences? We will discuss the personalization of beauty from various angles of technology, biotech, and big data. Join the event and be a part of the conversation. Stay until the end and see what surprise awaits you.

Discussion

1. How did the Ladies Who Tech get started and what's its original mission?
2. What'll happen on the coming April 29 according to the passage?

Part Two

Act out the following dialogs with your partner. Change the role when necessary.

Susan: Why don't you start searching for a job? Our classmates have all begun.

David: I want something more challenging.

Susan: Like what?

David: To run my own business and be my own boss.

Susan: Why do you want to start your own business? Nowadays, students in your field can easily find a job.

David: Well, I dislike being controlled by others, and I don't want to start from the bottom of a corporate hierarchy.

Susan: I don't mean to discourage you, but do you know that most new businesses fail? Are you fully prepared?

David: Yes, I am. To mitigate the risk, I will start by opening a small online store to make my first fortune.

Susan: That's practical. The profits may be modest, but you won't have to spend too much on overhead expenses.

David: Exactly. I can work from home, saving on the cost of renting an office. And I won't need to hire additional staff unless I become extremely busy.

Susan: Great, that way, over time, you can gradually accumulate enough startup capital for your own company.

应用型大学英语文化口语教程

A: Hey, buddy, how's your job search going?

B: Don't mention it. Everything is a mess.

A: That doesn't sound good.

B: Well, what about you? I heard you were planning to start a college club. Is that true?

A: Yeah, I'm currently applying for a bank loan.

B: Wow! That must be exciting and challenging.

A: Would you like to join us?

B: Me?

A: Exactly! I think you're a genius when it comes to IT.

B: But what would I do in your club?

A: You know, the Internet has become a crucial business tool. You can lead the efforts in developing and managing our website.

B: Are you serious? That's the exact job I've been looking for.

A: Great! Let's do it together and enjoy success in the future.

Interviewer: Dr. Wilen, can you please explain what the Maker Movement is?

Dr. Wilen: It is a return to the DIY activities. A lot involves technology and the development of new products, encouraging entrepreneurship. Many people have been tinkering in their garages or kitchens with technology, and now it is becoming more open, organized, and a movement.

Interviewer: So, when did it start?

Dr. Wilen: It started around 2006, and then there was a fair called "The Maker Faire". Now there are global events and conferences called "Maker Con". You can create your own maker week full of activities and get-togethers.

Interviewer: Would you mind giving some examples of maker activities?

Dr. Wilen: Actually, a lot of this is a return to school where girls had home economics and guys had "shops". We used to make things when we were kids. Today, teachers are returning to this in the classroom but with technology. They use 3D printers to print cookies and icing, and prototypes instead of easy bake ovens. They use technology to have kids explore how to build new products like Lego sets. It is sort of a revisit to the garage start-up concept of the Bay Area in the 70s and 80s, where people would gather to tinker, build, and maybe develop a hot new product or start-up firm.

Interviewer: What are schools actually doing nowadays in relation to this?

Dr. Wilen: Many schools are embracing the Maker Movement. Today, schools are incorporating math and science into the classroom, or STEM. Many schools are leading this initiative at the elementary and high school levels, starting with 3D printing projects, then robotics, and making circuits. Some even have maker labs.

Interviewer: Can you share something about student camps?

Dr. Wilen: Absolutely! I am meeting smart kids who share a common interest in learning about technology and come to the Bay Area to learn. I am working with the Envision Experience, where the agenda includes everything from coding to artificial intelligence, developing a personal brand, and creating a maker portfolio that students may need for college admissions.

Interviewer: Do you have to attend events regularly?

Dr. Wilen: Actually, you can create your own. A colleague of mine was very excited to spend a weekend with his daughter at a robotics meet-up group event in Palo Alto. Parents and kids learned how to build robots together over the weekend. The beauty of it is that multiple generations learn together from each other, creating and producing things, especially technology-related items.

Interviewer: What about social media? Do makers like to share their work?

Dr. Wilen: I think Pinterest is a great example of a website that encourages people to post their DIY projects and explain how they made them. People can pin photos of their projects and share their ideas. I also like the site "Quirky", as it allows you to connect with potential users and customers before developing an idea. This way, you don't have to make assumptions about what they will like.

Part Three

Read the following useful expressions and finish the matching exercise that follows.

- a challenging job 一份具有挑战性的工作
- a decent job 一份体面的工作
- a fat salary 收入颇丰
- a harmonious interpersonal relationship 和谐的人际关系
- a sense of accomplishment 成就感
- a sense of responsibility 责任感
- a sense of self-fulfillment 自我实现感
- a well-paid job 高收入工作
- accumulate experience 积累经验
- adapt oneself to… 使自己适应……
- adaptability 适应性
- ambitious 野心勃勃的
- arena 舞台
- balance work and life 平衡工作和生活
- be closely related to… 与……息息相关
- bright prospect 光明的前景
- chance of promotion 升迁机会
- company philosophy 公司理念
- competitive 竞争激烈的
- creative work 创造性工作
- cultivate one's independence and toughness 培养自己的独立性和坚韧性
- define one's role 找到自己的定位
- develop one's talent 培养才能
- display one's talent 展示才能

- DIY culture "自己动手做"的文化
- enrich one's social experience 丰富一个人的社会阅历
- expand one's horizon 开阔视野
- flexibility 灵活性
- flow of personnel 人才流动
- from nine to five 朝九晚五
- get advanced in the society 出人头地
- ideal workplace 理想工作场所
- improve one's capabilities 提高能力
- inspiring 鼓舞人心的
- keep skills fresh and up-to-date 不断更新技能
- learn to cooperate and compromise 学习合作和妥协
- master interpersonal skills 掌握人际交往技能
- material gains 物质待遇
- mechanism of personnel flow 人才流动机制
- meet one's personalized needs 满足个性化需求
- motivation 动机
- potentiality 潜能
- promising future 光明的前途
- promotion opportunity 提升机会
- prosperity 繁荣
- realize the value of life 实现人生价值
- seek for personal development 追求个人发展
- shoulder/undertake one's responsibility 承担责任
- social recognition 社会认可
- stability and satisfaction 稳定感和满足感
- stand up to/meet the challenge 迎接挑战
- survival of the fittest 适者生存

- team-work spirit 团队合作精神
- technology-based 基于技术的
- treasure opportunity 珍惜机会
- turning point 转折点
- upgrade oneself 提升自我
- work overtime 加班
- workaholic 工作狂
- working environment 工作环境
- A couple of months later, the Chinese term for maker—*chuangke*（创客）—had surged from hundreds to over three thousand hits per week on the search engine Baidu. 几个月后，"创客"一词在搜索引擎百度上的点击量从每周数百次飙升至超过三千次。
- A maker refers to a person who turns inventive ideas into reality out of his or her interest or love. 创客是指出于兴趣爱好，努力把各种创意转变为现实的人。
- By the time Maker Faire Shenzhen 2018 rolled around, held in tandem with the official National Mass Entrepreneurship and Innovation Week, a citywide map created by event organizers tallied 236 makerspaces in Shenzhen alone. 当2018年，深圳创客大会与官方的"全国大众创业和创新周"同时举行时，活动组织者创建的全市地图光在深圳就统计出了 236 个创客空间。
- China's Maker Movement takes root in the classroom. 中国的创客运动起源于课堂。
- Every week, Simpson tells us that he meets with a teacher in Dongguan to talk Dongguan about the techniques their staff can implement in the classroom. 辛普森告诉我们，每周他都会与东莞的老师见面，讨论他们的员工可以在课堂上实施的技术。
- Instructor Jane Liang gushes with enthusiasm when she talks about StreamHead, which has seen 40 kids sign up so far: "In terms of acceptance and the hands-on aspects, the kids have been excellent." 教师简·梁在谈到

StreamHead（到目前为止，已有 40 个孩子报名参加）时热情高涨："就接受度和动手方面而言，孩子们非常出色。"

- Interest in the DIY philosophy first peaked in January 2015, when Premier Li Keqiang toured Shenzhen's Chaihuo Makerspace and declared makers "an inexhaustible engine for China's future economic growth". 人们对 DIY 理念产生兴趣是在 2015 年 1 月首次达到顶峰，当时李克强总理参观了深圳的 Chaihuo 创客空间，并宣布创客是"中国未来经济增长取之不尽、用之不竭的引擎"。

- Leslie Liao is head of Maker Education Services for Chaihuo, the space that was highlighted by Li Keqiang's 2015 visit to Shenzhen. On the sidelines of this year's Maker Faire, he told TechNode that maker education is "methods and techniques combined with learning in order to solve problems". In other words, kids will get better skills to cope with a constantly changing world. Leslie Liao 是 Chaihuo 的创客教育服务负责人，2015 年李克强访问深圳时提到过这一空间。在今年的创客大会期间，他告诉 TechNode，创客教育是指"将方法和技术与学习相结合，以解决问题"。换句话说，孩子们将获得更好的技能来应对不断变化的世界。

- Amidst the burgeoning innovation ecosystem, the city unveiled plans to establish a network of state-of-the-art maker spaces, aiming to foster creativity and entrepreneurship among its citizens. 在不断蓬勃发展的创新生态系统中，该城市公布了建立一系列最先进的创客空间的计划，旨在培育市民的创造力和企业精神。

- The makerspace she helped found, StreamHead, is currently working together with Shenzhen's Dongguan Elementary School to offer a maker club for its students, many of whom are the children of migrants. 她帮助创立的创客空间 StreamHead 目前正在与深圳东莞小学合作，为其学生提供创客俱乐部，其中许多学生是移民的后代。

- Unlike at some other schools, where parents might lead the charge toward new ways of teaching, Dongguan's students have taken the initiative to get involved with StreamHead. 与其他一些学校不同,家长可能会寻求新的教学方式, 东莞的学生主动参与了 StreamHead 的项目。

- We have seen makers coming thick and fast. 众多创客脱颖而出。

Exercise

1. company philosophy   **A.** 朝九晚五
2. get advanced in the society   **B.** 升迁机会
3. from nine to five   **C.** 平衡工作和生活
4. flow of personnel   **D.** 光明的前途
5. chance of promotion   **E.** 公司理念
6. expand one's horizon   **F.** 自我实现感
7. balance work and life   **G.** 工作狂
8. promising future   **H.** 开阔视野
9. a sense of self-fulfillment   **I.** 出人头地
10. workaholic   **J.** 人才流动

Section B Picture-Related Description

Look at the following pictures and learn how to describe them.

 Maker Faire

Maker Faire is a vibrant gathering that celebrates the innovative spirit of creators, tinkerers, and inventors from diverse backgrounds. At Maker Faire, attendees can immerse themselves in hands-on activities, workshops, and demonstrations. They can explore innovative projects, interact with makers, and learn new skills. From robotics and

electronics to art and crafts, there's something for everyone to discover and be inspired by. Maker Faire offers a dynamic environment where creativity thrives, fostering a sense of community and collaboration among participants.

 Boxed Kits for Kids

Start-ups like Shenzhen's MG Space have flourished due to the demand for a maker education. The company began by selling boxed kits for kids to learn how to assemble their own toys and gadgets. It's the kind of prepackaged product that, in its most cookie-cutter form, has received criticism for stifling creativity. But MG has come full circle: After it started offering

classes, some students have used in-house parts to design and assemble their own creative "kits". One box for a "cross-country robot" contains a set of wooden parts and glue sticks, while another includes the basic hardware for a jittering, battery-powered buglike toy.

3 ## Parents and Kids Crafting Together

Parents of MG students agree that a maker education is good for "fostering interest" in practical things and it might be an "advantage" for the future. One of the parents is so enthused about the subject that she transferred her son from a traditional school to a new one precisely for its makerspace program. Since her son has always been a hands-on learner and an active child, she wanted to keep him interested in education while developing his critical thinking skills. Now her son is taking coding classes and has recently crafted a spinning, light-up Christmas tree together with his mother.

 4 ## A Maker in Panzhihua

Mr. Ma Hongqiang, a teacher at the Art School of Panzhihua University, opened his Gaoyuanyun Art Studio in 2018. Each weekend lots of kids in the city gather here to do some creative work, and laughter and excitement in the air are the specific proof of how popular his studio is. From the picture we can see that the shelves in the showroom are full of children's work, and kids are trying some pottery work under the guidance of their own imagination. According to Mr. Ma, he aimed to pass on the idea as widely as possible that every kid is an inborn artist and their potential and creativity should be valued, exploited, and protected, maybe through pottery.

5   A Maker in Chengdu

Under the creative influence of Yu Chenrui, wood not only comes alive, but also tells incredible stories and draws an appreciative audience. With the crank of a handle, the push of a button, or the tug of a string, wooden figures in his creations move as if by magic. Yu, 29, is a maker of automata, self-propelled, artistic mechanical figures, in Chengdu, Sichuan

Province. Automata are built to look like humans or animals and give the illusion of being able to move on their own.

6   What Is a Makerspace?

A makerspace is a designated area of your classroom or school in which the students learn to use materials and tools to create something unique. Having a makerspace in a classroom is a fast-growing trend in education. Some people refer to this trend as the Maker Movement. There are lots of different ways to define a makerspace. Essentially a makerspace is a space designed and

dedicated to hands-on learning and creativity. The Maker Movement activities usually include the use of digital technology and involve designing and constructing real or virtual things.

7   What Is STEM?

STEM, in full science, technology, engineering, and mathematics, is a field and curriculum centered on education in these disciplines. The STEM acronym was introduced in 2001 by scientific administrators at the U.S. National Science Foundation (NSF). The organization

previously used the acronym SMET when referring to the career fields in those disciplines or a curriculum that integrated knowledge and skills from those fields. In 2001, American biologist Judith Ramaley, then assistant director of education and human resources at NSF, rearranged the words to form the STEM acronym.

 ## LEGO

LEGO, a type of plastic building-block toy, rose to massive popularity in the mid-20th century. It has been one of the most successful game brands in marketing history. LEGO blocks originated in the Billund, Denmark, workshop of Ole Kirk Christiansen, who began making wooden toys in 1932. Two years later, he named his company LEGO after the Danish phrase "leg godt" ("play well"). In 1949, LEGO produced its first plastic brick, a precursor to its signature brick with interlocking studs on the top and tubes on the bottom. It was patented in 1958 by Christiansen's son Godtfred Kirk, who replaced his father as the head of the company.

Section C   Oral Practice

Part One

Look at the following pictures and have a talk with your partner using the prompting words.

Fablab

Prompting words: digital fabrication laboratory; place; create; mentor invent; innovation; assemble; install; debug; turnkey solutions

Maker Faire

Prompting words: celebration; Maker Movement; showcase; tech enthusiasts; crafters; educators; food artisans; hobbyists; engineers; science clubs; commercial exhibitors; glimpse the future

119

3 DIY Philosophy

Prompting words: continued learning; complete projects; resourcefulness; independence; creative; patience; hand-crafted

4 STEAM

Prompting words: abbreviation; integrated approach; encourage; ask questions; connect the dots; problem solving; think creatively; innovative

 5   **TIC Era Global Maker Town**

Prompting words: Guangfo business circle; central axis; Qiandeng Lake; spirit of maker; industrial; commercial; educational; ecological; cultural; residential values

 6   **World Maker Robot Contest**

Prompting words: robotics competitions; researchers; students; enthusiasts; tremendous opportunities; learn; solving a task; participating teams; operate; robot construction; control

7 3D Printer

Prompting words: 3D solid objects; digital file; additive process; layers of material; cutting; hollowing; metal, plastic; milling machine; complex shapes

8 Jeff Bezos

Prompting words: American entrepreneur; e-commerce; founder; chief executive officer; Amazon.com; Dream Institute; Princeton University

Part Two

Engage in a discussion with your partner to explore the topic of the Maker Movement, and prepare a presentation.

1. **The Maker Movement is a global creative revolution that represents a return to our artisanal past before production tools were predominantly owned by large corporations. Currently, there are over 125 established communities of the Maker Movement worldwide.**
   - What defines "a maker"?
   - Do makers need to possess exceptional talent or intelligence?
   - What skills should a maker specialize in?

2. **In recent years, pioneering schools in cities such as Beijing, Shenzhen, Wenzhou, and Ningbo have embraced the maker spirit by launching experimental programs that emphasize making, inventing, and creativity. School maker spaces, maker carnivals, and student innovation contests have gained popularity.**
   - Can you provide examples of maker activities?
   - How do students benefit from maker education?
   - What can teachers, administrators, and parents do to create opportunities for expressive innovation in learning?

3. **The LEGO Foundation recently released the results of a five-year research initiative that examined the role of play in enhancing educational curricula. The study discovered that over the past few decades, educators worldwide have been actively working towards incorporating STEAM subjects into their teaching methodologies. The increasing importance of these subjects is driven by the rapid pace of innovation and the evolving job market.**
   - What's the positive impact of learning through play?
   - What are the essential characteristics of learning through play?
   - Can learning through play be effective for learners of all ages?

4. **Apple, Google, Microsoft, and Hewlett-Packard are just a few examples of the most famous tech companies that had humble beginnings in garages. However, they are by no means the only ones. The garage has become an integral part of Silicon Valley culture and has evolved into a symbol of innovation and experimentation.**

   - Where do Chinese makers start their businesses?
   - Are there any maker spaces in your city?
   - What functions do maker spaces serve?
   - What challenges do Chinese maker spaces face?

5. **After all these preparations, you are expected to make a presentation on the great achievements in the world about the Maker Movement in your class. You can use PPT slides in your presentation.**

Section D   Critical Thinking

Read the following passage that would help you better understand the related topic of this unit, and then discuss the questions.

The Benefits of the Maker Movement in Education

In this article, we'll be learning all about the Maker Movement and how its philosophy can be applied in educational settings.

The phrases "do it yourself" or "do it with others" are what identify the Maker Movement. This social movement has a close link to information and communication technologies (ICT). Its objective is to make and share knowledge regarding the use and development of technological devices and applications.

The Maker Movement: Doing

The Maker Movement is a subculture that promotes the idea that all of us can perform any task we want with the help of technology. So, in this way, the Maker Movement aims to get people to participate and share in the creative production of all kinds of devices.

The philosophy of the Maker Movement is that of people coming together in the spirit of "doing". In this context, they share experiences, skills, and knowledge. Students can carry this out through the use of hardware (electronic components) and software (programs that run on that hardware), as well as open-source code. These are all inexpensive, easily accessible, and shared.

This movement is aided by digital design and manufacturing tools. These include 3D printers and scanners, laser cutters, and design software for the manufacture of the devices. People can create everything from intelligent devices, robots, and drones, to clothes, food, cosmetics, and even music.

The Maker Movement in Education

The Maker Movement and its "do it yourself" or "do it with others" philosophy have positive aspects that we can apply in school settings. Maker culture can be adapted to education as a way of using and developing technological devices and applications. However, it can also be used as a way of learning concepts and increasing knowledge of school subjects or specific learning areas.

This is possible because it promotes the conceiving and organizing of learning through collaboration. At the same time, it helps promote understanding of concepts and operations. In this way, it also helps generate active, critical, creative, and supportive attitudes in students.

In the educational field, the Maker Movement can encourage meaningful learning, by the action of "doing". It also highlights the importance of active and interactive learning, both shared and collaborative. This is all based on creativity and fun. Above all, in relation to new technology, maker culture helps students become aware of the possibilities they have at their fingertips to create things. It doesn't only encourage the use of technology but also gives them the chance to develop advanced digital skills themselves. We should point out that this requires specific curriculum planning and teaching skills.

Conclusions

The Maker Movement in education brings great benefits when it comes to training students. It also has great potential to improve educational and pedagogical practices.

This is because, in the first place, it helps reaffirm the importance of education in order to learn to use technology. It also encourages digital media as the means of accessing information.

And, secondly, because it's in the actual classrooms that the learning encouraged by the Maker Movement is organized. This learning method is supported by technology. Not only is it based on using it, but also on making and doing things with it all in a creative, innovative, shared, and democratic way.

Discussion

1. How does the Maker Movement's emphasis on "do it yourself" and "do it with others" impact traditional educational approaches?
2. What are the potential benefits and drawbacks of incorporating the Maker Movement into educational practices?

Unit 6
Science and Technology

Learning Objectives

1. To acquire useful expressions used in oral tasks on science and technology;
2. To practice expressions for the related topic on science and technology;
3. To present your ideas on science and technology effectively;
4. To get more information about science and technology development in China.

Warm-up Questions

1 What technology in ancient China impresses you the most?
2 How does technology change our life?
3 What's the significance of science and technology development?

Section A   Getting Ready to Speak

Part One

Read the following topic-related passages and answer the questions accordingly.

Paper Making

Paper has been a major medium of recording, transmitting, and storing information in human civilization. The earliest characters were inscribed on bones, tortoise shells, and bronze wares in the Shang Dynasty and later on silk, bamboo, and wood. In particular, the bamboo slip has been used as a book form for the longest time in Chinese history. It was the main writing tool before the invention of paper-making and the popularization of paper.

In the Eastern Han Dynasty, a court official named Cai Lun used inexpensive materials such as bark, hemp, rags, fishnet, wheat stalks, and other materials to make paper, known as Cai Lun Paper.

Question 1: What were the earliest forms of writing used in human civilization?
Question 2: Who is credited with inventing paper, and what materials did he use to make it?

Printing

Printing, known as "the mother of civilization", was another great invention of the Chinese people. It has a long history and includes block printing and movable type printing.

Block printing (Carved plate printing) was probably invented between the Sui and Tang Dynasties. The process of block printing started with the cutting of wood into blocks, and then characters were engraved in relief on the blocks. Ink was brushed on the engraved block and a white sheet of paper was spread across it and then brushed with a clean brush on its back, leaving an image when the paper was removed.

Block printing was developed on the basis of ancient stone carving and seal carving. In the beginning of the Sui Dynasty, the Chinese people had already printed large numbers of religious pictures with carved plates. In the Tang Dynasty, the Chinese people had already printed a number of books in fairly wide circulation with carved plates. As the world's oldest surviving book printed on paper, *Diamond Sutra* (《金刚经》), discovered in Dunhuang Grottos, was printed in 868 A.D. in the Tang Dynasty.

Due to the high cost of carved plate printing concerning labor and material, the printing industry was set to improve the technique. In the Song Dynasty, Bi Shen, a printing carver, invented typography (凸版印刷术) or movable type printing.

Movable type printing involved engraving single words into pieces of clay, firing them until hardened, and using them as permanent types. The types were then set into printing plates. The pieces of movable types could be glued to an iron plate and easily detached from the plate. This was the beginning of typography. Later, people also made types with lead, tin, copper, and other metals.

Question 1: When was block printing likely invented?
Question 2: What inspired the development of block printing?

Gunpowder

Originally, gunpowder was used in China for making fireworks and firecrackers for the sake of amusement. In the Tang Dynasty, the gunpowder began to be applied in the military affairs.

During the Song and Yuan Dynasties, the military applications of gunpowder became common.

After the 13th century, gunpowder spread gradually to Arabia, and then to Europe. It was a tremendous impetus to the progress of European history. The invention of gunpowder meant a far-reaching technological revolution that transformed chemical energy into mechanical energy, greatly promoting the progress of global civilization.

Question 1: What was the original purpose of gunpowder in China?

Question 2: When did gunpowder start to be used for military purposes?

Part Two

Act out the following dialogs with your partner. Change the role when necessary.

A: Hi, good afternoon. How are you?

B: I'm fine. What have you been up to lately?

A: Our company is currently working on a new product!

B: Wow! That's exciting. How do you go about developing a new product?

A: Well, first and foremost, we need to come up with an idea.

B: Where do these ideas typically come from?

A: They come from various sources.

B: Can you give me an example?

A: Sure, many ideas come from our own research and development department.

B: That's a great approach. They are at the forefront of R&D, so their input is crucial. What else?

A: We also gather ideas from other employees within the company, our customers, focus groups, and by attending trade shows.

B: How do you ensure that the product you're developing will be competitive in the market?

A: We place great emphasis on quality and focus on developing innovative products.

B: So you have an idea. How do you test the feasibility?

A: First, we ask ourselves key questions about the ideas. Then, we conduct multiple rounds of

product testing. Ultimately, we aim for a 100% success rate.

B: That sounds great. I have confidence in your success.

A: Thank you.

B: See you later.

Tom: Hey, Bob, what are you up to?

Bob: I'm playing a game called *Warcraft*.

Tom: It seems like you're quite busy with it.

Bob: Yeah, I'm always caught up and can't find time to respond to my teammates in the game.

Tom: No worries, in the future, there will be even more interactive experiences between humans and PCs.

Bob: Can you give me some more details about that?

Tom: British scientists are currently conducting research on the integration of the real world and the virtual world. This technology will enable your PC or game console to recognize your expressions and respond accordingly.

Bob: Wow, that's really awesome!

Tom: Let's keep our hopes up for it.

Bob: I'm really looking forward to it!

Wei: Hey, what did you do yesterday evening? I called you, but you didn't answer.

La: Oh, I'm sorry. I was playing computer games. It was really enjoyable.

Wei: You're so unreliable.

La: Well, what's the matter? Why did you call me yesterday?

Wei: I wanted to discuss with you about technology. What's your opinion on its rapid development?

La: I believe that various technological advancements have brought great benefits to people's lives. For example, transportation has become safer, faster, more comfortable, and more convenient with the emergence of new modes of transportation. Even the shipping of goods has become faster and more affordable.

Wei: However, more and more people have become overly dependent on technology. Although cars offer convenience for travelling, they have led to serious traffic congestion issues.

La: Don't be so pessimistic. Thanks to technology, people have seen significant improvements in both workspaces and living conditions. Buildings are now more environmentally-friendly and energy-efficient. Look at our beautiful new teaching building!

Wei: But have you noticed that the sky has never looked so blue? Industrial emissions have polluted the air, making it harder for people to breathe and contributing to the greenhouse effect and global warming.

La: Okay, every coin has two sides. The rapid development of technology is a double-edged sword. It's hard to determine whether it's good or bad. Let's go and grab some lunch.

Part Three

Read the following useful expressions and finish the matching exercise that follows.

- a wide variety of 很多的
- aim to do something 指望做某事
- artificial intelligence 人工智能
- at high altitudes 在很高的地方
- automation 自动化
- be curious about... 对……感到好奇
- be on the verge of extinction 处于灭绝的边缘
- carry out 完成
- communication technology 通信科技
- confront with 面临
- depletion of resources 能源的损耗
- distance education 远程教育
- electric appliance 电器
- electronic device 电子设备
- endangered species 濒危物种
- energy crisis 能源危机
- environment deterioration 环境恶化
- global warming 全球变暖
- high-tech facilities/products 高科技设施/产品
- home working/telecommuting work 在家办公
- hostile environment 恶劣的环境
- household appliance 家用电器
- hybrid rice 杂交水稻
- in the long run 从长远来看

- information age 信息时代
- life expectancy/span 寿命
- live TV broadcast 现场直播
- make sacrifices 做出牺牲
- manned spaceship/spacecraft 载人飞船
- mass manufacture 大量生产
- mechanical labor 机械劳动
- modern technology 现代科技
- moon landing 登月
- national security 国家安全
- natural resources 天然资源
- navigation system 导航系统
- nuclear weapon 核武器
- promote the development of human society 促进人类社会的发展
- renewable energy sources 可再生资源
- scientific achievement 科学成就
- scientific instrument 科学仪器
- sci-tech civilization 科技文明
- set apart from 把……区分开
- set foot on 踏足于
- Shenzhou VI spacecraft 神舟六号
- space exploration/research 太空研究
- technological advancement/development 技术进步
- technological innovation 科技创新
- the fast rhythm of life 快节奏的生活方式
- the widespread use of the Internet 网络的广泛使用
- A nation without innovation ability can hardly stand in the forest of advanced nations in the world. 一个没有创新能力的民族，难以屹立于世界先进民族之林。

- Innovation is a creative destruction. 创新是一种创造性的破坏。

- Innovation is the soul and talent is the foundation. 创新是魂，人才是本。

- Innovation is the soul of a nation's progress and the inexhaustible motive force for the country's prosperity. 创新是一个民族进步的灵魂，是国家兴旺发达的不竭动力。

- Innovation needs to break the stereotype, the breakthrough tradition. 创新需要打破定势，突破传统。

- Knowledge is a treasure, but practice is the key to it. 知识是宝库，而实践是开启宝库大门的钥匙。

- Nothing is difficult to the man who will try. 世上无难事，只要肯登攀。

- Science and art are two sides of a coin. 科学和艺术是一枚硬币的两面。

- Science and technology are the primary productive force. 科学技术是第一生产力。

- Science has no borders, but scholars have their own countries. 科学虽没有国界，但是学者却拥有不同的国籍。

- The beam of science and technology lights up your appearance but ignores the feeling of the heart. 科技的光束照亮了人们的外表，却忽略了内心的感受。

- The development of high technology is indeed a double-edged sword. 高科技的发展确实是一把双刃剑。

- The pursuit of science needs special courage. 追求科学需要格外的勇气。

- The question mark is the key to any science. 问号是开启任何一门科学的钥匙。

- Thought is the ruler of the universe forever. 思想永远是宇宙的统治者。

- Well begun is half done. 良好的开端是成功的一半。

- Where there is a will, there is a way. 有志者，事竟成。

- With the rapid development of hi-tech, our life will change a lot in many ways in the future. 随着高科技的飞速发展，未来我们的生活将在很多方面发生很大的变化。

Exercise

1.	confront with	A.	把……区分开
2.	depletion of resources	B.	人工智能
3.	distance education	C.	使面临
4.	set apart from	D.	从长远来看
5.	set foot on	E.	能源的损耗
6.	hybrid rice	F.	远程教育
7.	in the long run	G.	踏足于
8.	artificial intelligence	H.	做出牺牲
9.	be on the verge of extinction	I.	杂交水稻
10.	make sacrifices	J.	处于灭绝的边缘

Section B   Picture-Related Description

Look at the following pictures and learn how to describe them.

Compass

Early in the Spring and Autumn Period, while mining ores and melting copper and iron, Chinese people chanced upon a natural magnetite that attracted iron and pointed fixedly north. In the Warring States Period, referred to as a "south-pointer", the spoon or ladle-shaped compass is made of magnetic lodestone, and the plate is bronze. The compass in the real

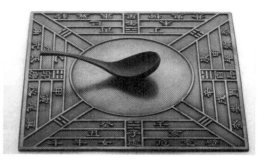

sense was created in the late Tang Dynasty. The major material of the compass is a magnetized steel needle, making up for the flaw that magnetism is easily lost in lodestones, of which Si'nan was made.

Calendar

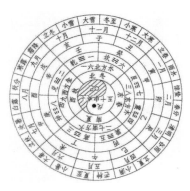

Ancient Chinese astronomy laid the foundation for the Chinese calendar, derived from the sun's longitude, moon phases, and defining days, months, and years. The traditional Chinese calendar is called the "Agricultural Calendar", while the Gregorian calendar is the "Common Calendar". It's also known as the "yin calendar" due to its lunar aspects, in contrast to the "yang calendar" of the Gregorian system. Today, the Gregorian calendar is used for daily life, while the Chinese calendar remains for traditional holidays and selecting auspicious dates for events like weddings and building openings. This transition leads to the Chinese calendar being referred to as the "old calendar", with the Gregorian calendar as the "new calendar", which is now the official.

3 Solar Term

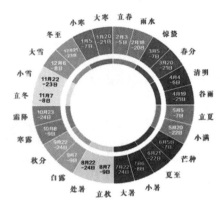

A solar term is any of the 24 points in the traditional Chinese calendar that matches a particular astronomical event or signifies some natural phenomenon. It made great contributions to agriculture. Ancient Chinese created it by using sundials. They decided the day with the shortest sun shadow as Winter Solstice, and the day with the longest shadow as Summer Solstice.

4 Abacus

An abacus is a form of manual computing instrument. It has a history of more than 2,600 years, and is an important invention in ancient China. Before the advent of Arab numbers, the abacus was widely used as a computing tool in the world.

5 Shenzhou V

Shenzhou V manned spacecraft is the fifth of the Shenzhou spacecraft series. It is the first manned spacecraft launched by China. It was launched at 9:00 on October 15, 2003, at Jiuquan Satellite Launch Center, sending astronaut Yang Liwei and a Chinese flag of special significance into space. It returned at 6:23 on October 16, 2003. The spacecraft marks China as the third country to send humans into space after Russia and the United States. It also marks another milestone in China's aerospace technology.

6 Atomic Bomb

After 1949, in order to build a strong national defense and not be bullied by imperialism, China began to build a nuclear industry in 1955. In 1959, the Soviet Union withdrew its experts who supported China, and China began to develop its nuclear industry on its own. In 1962, China established a special leading organization headed by Premier Zhou Enlai to be responsible for the research and development of the atomic bomb. With everyone's efforts, in that difficult era, China's nuclear test was finally successful. At 3:00 p.m. on October 16, 1964, the first atomic bomb developed by China successfully exploded in Lop Nor, Xinjiang, becoming the fifth country in the world to possess nuclear weapons after the United States, the Soviet Union, Britain, and France.

7 Chengdu–Chongqing Railway

On July 1, 1952, the Chengdu–Chongqing Railway, the first railway built by China, was opened to traffic. This is China's first railway completely designed and built by itself with all materials and parts made in China. The total length of the route is 505 kilometers. The railway starts from Chengdu, Sichuan Province in the northwest and ends in Chongqing. This is an unimaginable miracle in any era before 1949 and an initiative in the history of Chinese railways. The completion of the Chengdu–Chongqing Railway has great economic values. It crosses the center of the Sichuan Basin and effectively promotes material exchange in southwest China.

8 The Father of the Hybrid Rice

Yuan Longping was born in Beijing on September 7, 1930. His ancestral home is De'an, Jiangxi Province. He once studied in Southwest Agricultural College (renamed Southwest Agricultural University in 1985). Academician Yuan Longping is an outstanding contemporary agricultural scientist in China and the world-famous "father of hybrid rice". In 1973, Yuan Longping bred indica hybrid rice for the first time in the world. After continuous efforts, he successfully cultivated the "three-line hybrid rice". Now, it is widely planted in farmland in the north and south of China. His scientific research achievements have led China to the world level in the field of hybrid rice research and application. After its popularization and application, he has not only solved the problem of China's food self-sufficiency but also made outstanding contributions to the world's food security.

Section C　Oral Practice

Part One

Look at the following pictures and have a talk with your partner using the prompting words.

1 Shenzhou XII

Prompting words: space station; spaceship; Jiuquan Satellite Launch Center; launch satellite; lift off; ignition; blast off

2 On a Space Mission

Prompting words: core module; capsule; mission control; manned space mission; taikonaut; crew; prime crew; commander

3 **Tiangong Space Station**

Prompting words: Tiangong (Heavenly Palace); space station; perform two spacewalks; stay in orbit for three months

 4 **China's Mars Rover Zhurong**

Prompting words: China's Mars Rover Zhurong; Mars orbiter; Martian days; subsurface radar; meteorological measuring instrument; detection

5 Driverless Bus

Prompting words: self-driving vehicle; use cutting-edge technologies; optimize the transportation networks; expansion of unmanned public transportation operations

6 China's Easternmost High-Speed Railway

Prompting words: China's easternmost high-speed railway; test operations; endure extremely cold temperatures; cover 95% of populous cities

7 **China's HongKong–Zhuhai–Macao Bridge**

Prompting words: the world's longest cross-sea bridge; stretch 55 kilometers; a 22.9-kilometer steel bridge, artificial islands; undersea tunnel; span

 8 **5G**

Prompting words: trigger; essential breakthroughs; superfast; wireless technology; smart cities

Part Two

Engage in a discussion with your partner to explore the topic of science and technology, and prepare a presentation.

1. **Every Chinese feels a sense of pride when discussing our nation's space achievements with friends. To start the conversation, you can delve into the history of China's space industry development and share some noteworthy stories. Here are a few key points for your talk to include:**
    *   The history of China's space industry development.
    *   Famous figures who have dedicated themselves to China's space industry.

2. **Suppose you are the host assigned to interview the taikonauts, and the questions for the interview can be as follows:**
    *   Launch day is a time filled with excitement for everyone, but also with anxieties about the risks and the fear that may arise within us. How do you prepare for launch day?
    *   During each launch, I find myself holding my breath, and I'm sure many others do too. We are curious to know how you manage to strike a balance between being aware of the risks and remaining calm enough to carry out your duties.
    *   How would you describe the personal changes you have experienced from being away from the Earth?

3. **The Hong Kong–Zhuhai–Macao Bridge, the longest cross-sea bridge globally, connects the eastern and western sides of the Pearl River Delta in the southern region. It was designed and constructed by the Chinese. When discussing this bridge with your partner, you may consider the following questions:**
    *   Are there any famous ancient bridges in your hometown?
    *   Show pictures of the Hong Kong–Zhuhai–Macao Bridge to your friends and provide an introduction that sparks their curiosity about more details.

4. **The rapid development of science and technology has brought about significant changes to human life. The immense benefits resulting from this progress have been celebrated worldwide. When discussing technologies that have transformed your lifestyle, consider the following points:**

   - Introduce a new gadget that has significantly impacted your life to your partner.
   - Discuss the benefits that this gadget has brought to you personally.

5. **After all these preparations, design a presentation and present the great achievements of China to your class. You can use PPT slides in your presentation.**

Section D   Critical Thinking

Read the following passage that would help you better understand the related topic of this unit, and then discuss the questions.

Successful Programs Ignited by Modest Spark of an Idea

It was in August 1958 that Chinese scientists started to float the idea of sending Chinese astronauts to space.

At that time, the Chinese Academy of Sciences (CAS), the country's top scientific body, had formed a panel of distinguished scientists to discuss the research and development of satellites. Whether and how China should start a manned space program was also included on the agenda, three years before the Soviet Union's Yuri Gagarin undertook mankind's first space journey.

During a workshop at the Academy's Institute of Mechanics in Beijing in late August, Zhao Jiuzhang, a preeminent geophysicist, became the first Chinese scientist to suggest the government consider developing and building spaceships for manned missions. Meanwhile, a handful of Chinese institutes had also begun to carry out preliminary research in the fields related to manned spaceflights, such as life-support technologies.

With a mountain of difficulties facing the young People's Republic of China, the government and the scientific community soon found that they could not afford the resources required for a manned space program, and would have to bide their time.

In February 1963, the CAS established a "space travel commission" to make theoretical preparations for robotic and manned spaceflights.

In the next three years, several remarkable advances were made: Two institutes were founded to prepare for manned space missions; specific schedules were produced; and scientists launched several carrier rockets to ferry animals, including dogs and monkeys into and back from space.

Although endeavors by mission planners and scientists slowed down during the period of the "Cultural Revolution", they did not abandon their aspirations to send Chinese into space and continued trying to persuade the government to approve and fund a manned spaceflight.

In February 1968, the government set up the People's Liberation Army (PLA) Fifth Academy, which later became the China Academy of Space Technology, to design and manufacture satellites and also to explore manned spaceship technologies. In the meantime, more researchers from around the country began to take part in discussions and planning for China's first manned spacecraft, which was named by state leaders Shuguang 1, or Dawn Light 1.

In July 1970, Chairman Mao Zedong and other top leaders formally approved China's first manned space program. Three months later, the PLA started to select 20 astronaut candidates from Air Force pilots and train them at a highly classified complex in Beijing.

The government had also chosen a remote valley in Xichang, Sichuan Province, as the location of a new space launch facility to serve manned spaceflights. The facility's construction started in the winter of 1970.

Due to the nation's poor technological and industrial capabilities as well as the absence of institutes and factories capable of making certain components, China's manned spaceflight program halted in the mid-1970s.

About 10 years later, space authorities and scientists urged the government to reopen the program and add a new objective: to build a permanent space station.

In the 1980s, their suggestion became a reality as the government launched what later became known as Project 863.

In August 1992, a special committee decided that China would use manned spacecraft to assemble a space station in the near future. The plan was approved in September that year by the top leadership, officially kicking off the nation's manned space exploration program.

Discussion

1.　Can you tell the history of China's space industry development and some noteworthy stories in your own words?
2.　Can you talk about how advanced space technology benefits mankind?

教师服务

感谢您选用清华大学出版社的教材！为了更好地服务教学，我们为授课教师提供本学科重点教材信息及样书，请您扫码获取。

≫ 最新书目

扫码获取 2024 **外语类**重点教材信息

≫ 样书赠送

教师扫码即可获取样书